The World of Comedy

The World of Comedy

Thomas Leeflang

Translated by Phil Goddard

WINDWARD

This edition published 1988 by
WINDWARD
an imprint owned by WH Smith & Son Ltd
Registered No. 237811 England Trading as WHS Distributors
St Johns House, East Street, Leicester LE1 6NE

The World of Comedy was produced by Bookworld
International Ltd for Windward

This edition copyright © Bookworld International Ltd 1988

Design and editorial by Mackenzie Publishing Limited
Layout and artwork by Keith Smith
Translation by AGET Language Services

First published in the Netherlands as De wereld van de
comedy by Unieboek B.V. © Unieboek B.V. 1985

ISBN 0711 204 934

Typeset by Keene Graphics, London
Printed in Spain by Artes Graficas Toledo SA.
D. L. TO: 367-1988

Comedy is the satire of tragedy.
Harry Langdon (1884-1944)

Contents

Introduction

When Mack Sennett, 'The King of Comedy', was buried in November 1960 at the age of eighty, he was poor and almost forgotten by the public. This was the man who pioneered slapstick comedy, created such great comedy teams as the Keystone Cops and the Bathing Beauties and found hitherto undreamed-of uses for the humble custard pie.

This combination of *pâtisserie* and *policierie* was an absurd one, but Sennett was nevertheless regarded as a shrewd businessman. However, in 1935 his studio went bankrupt and he never managed to regain his important position in the film industry after the demise of the silent film. Mack Sennett was the prototype of the Hollywood personality who made it to the top and then failed completely. Just before he died he was forced to sell the movie camera he had been given as a present when he was the subject of a 'This is Your Life' programme on NBC in 1954. Many local and national TV stations had a short season of Mack Sennett films in tribute, but these received hardly any attention from the viewing public. The fact was that the great classics of slapstick do not lend themselves to viewing by small numbers of people at a time. It takes the noisy, pleasured anticipation of a large cinema audience to make one really appreciate any of the great silent classics: on your own, or with a handful of others in front of a TV screen at home, the film simply fails to work its magic. Today's generation is beginning to see these silent black-and-white films as relics of a bygone era. Many attempts have been made to revive them by putting them together in compilations, adding a soundtrack, including interviews or even, in the United States, using computer technology to turn black-and-white films into colour ones. But the fact remains that the average TV viewer is starting to get bored with silent comedy.

Mack Sennett, the 'King of Silent Comedy' (1917).

The Bathing Beauties, formed by Mack Sennett in 1916 to add sex appeal to his comedies.

When the word 'comedy' is mentioned, many people automatically think of the Americans. Although some of the great comic geniuses of the cinema were at work outside the United States (George Formby in England, Fernandel and Jacques Tati in France and Karl Valentin in Germany), it was primarily Hollywood that fed the appetites of European filmgoers from about 1920 onwards, and all the more so when television started to make its influence felt.

Television created a whole new market for comedy films of between half an hour and an hour in length, usually in serial form. This became the standard length from 1948 onwards when film studios such as Columbia, Monogram, Republic and the studios of the Crown Prince of Comedy, Hal Roach (the successor to Mack Sennett) began selling their old B-movies and two- and three-reel comedies cheaply to the television companies. It was not until this time that the American comedians of the thirties, forties and early fifties started to become really famous throughout the world. Laurel and Hardy were rediscovered when their films started to be shown frequently on TV. The same is also true of the Three Stooges, Harold Lloyd, Abbott and Costello, W. C. Fields and the Marx Brothers. Even the more recent comedians Dean Martin and Jerry Lewis somehow seem funnier on the small screen than when they were working with Paramount between 1949 and 1956.

Nowadays, television itself is growing and maturing as a medium and television comedians have joined the ranks of the great classics. Lucille Ball, for example, has earned the title 'Queen of Comedy'. From October 1951 to September 1974 (with one two-year break) this red-haired 'charming clown' produced one sitcom a week for CBS. Her three series, 'I Love Lucy', 'The Lucy Show' and 'Here's Lucy' were shown in twenty-eight countries and reruns can still be seen on the world's television screens. The older Lucille Ball's shows become, the more they seem to gain in attraction, particularly those recorded in black and white. Old they may be, but they have retained their freshness and originality in a way that some of the slapstick comedies of the 1920s have failed to do.

What applies to the world's most widely exported TV series, Lucille Ball's, is equally true of the comedies produced during what has become known as the Golden Age of Hollywood. These films return to the television screen time and time again, where they provide amusement for a younger generation and nostalgic pleasure for an older.

Whilst American cinema produced many unarguably great masterpieces (*Gone With the Wind, Citizen Kane, Stagecoach* and *The Grapes of Wrath,* to name but a few), it is more often than not the simple, unpretentious but beautifully made minor films which are remembered by the public: Johnny Weissmuller in *Tarzan the Ape Man,* Roy Rogers in *My Pal Trigger,* Maria Montez in *Cobra Woman* and the Mr Moto films with Peter Lorre. And first and foremost it is the comedies which have captured people's imaginations: Abbott and Costello in *Hit the Ice,* the Three Stooges in *Rockin' in the Rockies,* W. C. Fields in *My Little Chickadee,* Martin and Lewis in *Sailor Beware,* Laurel and Hardy in *Way Out West* and the Marx Brothers in *Animal Crackers.*

As will be seen from the above, the comedians discussed in this book are all American , some possibly better known to the reader than others. The book gave me a great deal of pleasure to write and is an expression of affectionate respect for popular cinema. There may not be much to cinema comedy, but it is an expression of hope. Although virtually no art form has received greater publicity and attention than the film, there is much that still remains to be discovered and a great deal of intellectual debate still surrounds it. Often it becomes difficult to separate fact from fiction, and old wives' tales about the cinema are recounted as fact. Many of the studios have been pulled down and the comedians, directors and producers are long dead, or if still alive are too old to be the source of any new or relevant information. So our examination of the history of film comedy must be made on the basis of the films themselves and on the letters, books and documents we still have available.

Film director Frank Capra, who worked for Mack Sennett for a short time, says in his autobiography, *The Name Above the Title* (Macmillan, New York, 1971): 'Mack Sennett had a tremendous library of books. When I finally looked at one, the leaves had never been cut. He just bought them by the yard!'

Details like this one give a nice picture of the man, one which is sharper and clearer than the bald facts given in the average film encyclopaedias: *i/Sennett, Mack. 1884-1960. One of the first people to make pictures',* followed by his unpredictable and inspiring life history.

Stan Laurel and Oliver Hardy
in *Our Relations* (1936).

All that we know about the early American film industry, its
actors, directors, scriptwriters, studios and so on, has been put down in
writing already by other people. It is often difficult to separate the wheat
from the chaff amongst this flood of information, and some authors of
books on the cinema appear to be claiming to understand the films they
are writing about better than the people who actually made them. There
has been a great deal of literature which purports to show that there is
more in some of these films than even the makers realized at the time.

In this book we hope to steer clear of this approach. It is not a
wrong approach, and of course it is perfectly possible for one person to
see a film in a different light to another. The problem lies in defining
precisely what we mean by a comedy. For example, when does a
musical with a few comic scenes in it become a comedy? And
conversely, if a comedy contains musical scenes, at what point does it
start to be a musical? And for that matter, why does one film make us
laugh and another not? What techniques are available to the comedian
to reach out from the television or cinema screen and make the audience
laugh? Throwing a custard pie at someone's face? A deckchair that
refuses to unfold into anything that can actually be sat on? A
bubblegum machine that refuses to deliver the goods? A bar of soap
that slips out of Stan Laurel's hands and causes Oliver Hardy to fall over
with a pile of newly washed crockery? No satisfactory definition of
what is truly comic and what is not has yet been provided.

When comedian Jerry Lewis was interviewed by *American Film* magazine in September 1979, he said, 'That's why the things that are written about comedy frustrate me, because people don't know what the hell they are talking about!'

In the same article, Jerry Lewis says that he once asked Stan Laurel, the great genius of film comedy, whether there was any definition of what was 'funny' and what was not. Said Laurel to his younger colleague: 'I wish I could tell you what comedy is, I don't know.'

So we will make no attempt in this book to decide why Harold Lloyd is funny or what makes a crooked bowler hat amusing. The fact is that most comedians make people laugh. There is an almost magical element in the way Laurel and Hardy go about doing so, helped by the fact that the audience knows and loves the two actors. Or take a more recent comedian, Woody Allen, whose comic genius often sends his audiences home from the cinema aching with laughter. In 1983, Allen made his fictional biography of the chamaeleon man, his own pseudo-historical *alter ego*. *Zelig* is set in the 1930s intercut with scenes from genuine documentaries. Zelig himself appears in any number of different disguises, often at historical events which actually took place. At the Nazi conference in Nuremberg he is the SS man bobbing up and down, panic-stricken, behind the Führer. Using the latest cinematic techniques, Allen himself is made to appear in a film made by Leni Riefenstahl, the great Nazi documentary film maker. Allen assumes countless different personalities during the course of the film (see the chapter on Woody Allen in this book). A funny film? Opinions have varied, but Rex Reed, one of the world's most revered critics, writing in the *New York Post,* said after the première: 'Woody Allen is America's most brilliantly funny man. *Zelig* is a work of pure genius. A movie unlike anything you have seen before. There is no other movie in history like *Zelig*. Diabolically hilarious!' But other critics were left totally unmoved by the film, finding it little more than a piece of clever cinematic artifice: just because some regard a film as a masterpiece does not mean that everyone will.

The following chapters will introduce, or help you renew your acquaintance if you know them already, the comedies which came out of Hollywood in the twenties, thirties, forties and fifties or, more specifically, the period between about 1925 and 1955. During these three decades, the American 'fun factory' produced large quantities of film comedies almost continuously. They were made with skill and professionalism, the makers never thinking for a moment that they would still have any appeal half a century after they were made. The average 'life' of a film in those days was from one to five years. Although actors and actresses achieved considerable fame amongst the cinema-going public, their fame was nothing compared to the renown they would achieve later on when their films were shown on television. Many of them did not achieve true international recognition until the last few years of their lives, and most are better known and more popular now than when they were actually making films.

The filmographies which appear at the end of the book may not always be complete, as some films were given new titles later on and it is difficult to be truly comprehensive, but they should be useful as a guide to watching the comedies on television. It is better to have a filmography of a particular comedian which is not quite complete than none at all, and any omissions should become apparent as the reader sees the films.

I hope, even if the reader does not read all the text, that the photographs (all original stills from my collection) will give as much pleasure as they give me. They are icons from Hollywood, where from a cinematic point of view the past looks a great deal more attractive than the future.

Harpo Marx in a scene with Red Skelton made for CBS TV in 1962.

1

Abbott and Costello: Radio comedy on the cinema screen

The first American film comedian was Fred Ott. Unfortunately, he never achieved world renown. Ott worked with William K.L. Dickson, who was assistant to the inventor Thomas Edison and was making 'films' for the Kinetoscope Company in the Black Maria studio in West Orange, New Jersey in 1894. These were not films in the sense in which we understand them, but were made for the Kinetoscope, a coin-operated device which flashed pictures in front of the viewer to give the appearance of motion. Until this time, these peepshow devices were the only way of seeing 'moving pictures'.

The films consisted mainly of boxing matches, belly dancers and gymnastic displays of various kinds. Fred Ott's ability lay in the fact that he was able to sneeze on demand. Amongst all the mainly serious Kinetoscope films, Fred Ott acted as comic relief, and he actually achieved some renown as a comedian for this reason.

At the turn of the century, people in the United States who wanted a good laugh could go to fairs, or theatre shows with a strong parody content (burlesque), or a combination of sketches and often quite *risqué* songs (vaudeville), or a colourful evening's juggling, conjuring, singing and dancing in the form of a variety show. Equally, they might go to a circus or a showboat.

Between 1910 and 1925, many ambitious artists from these various fields of entertainment beat a path to the film studios, for this new artistic medium had room for almost anyone who was willing and able to take part. The studios were desperate for new, original talent and there were soon many of them: Inspiration Pictures, Vitagraph Studios, Lasky Studios, Mack Sennett Studios, Distinctive Productions, Hal Roach Studios, Fox Studios, Griffith Studios, Paramount Studios and Metro Studios, to name but a few.

On 8 June 1912, a German former fabric merchant, Carl Laemmle, set up a new studio at 1 Union Street in New York City. Laemmle was director of the Independent Motion Picture Company of America and the studio was established in conjuction with Pat Bowers Picture Plays and Bison Life Motion Pictures. The story goes that 'Uncle' Carl stood

Hit the Ice (1943), Abbott and Costello's eleventh feature film.

up and looked out of the window after signing the necessary documents, and as he did so a lorry drove past bearing the name 'Universal Pipe Fittings'. So the studio became known as the Universal Film Manufacturing Company, and it still exists today, being particularly active in the television industry. It has always striven to produce good, inexpensive films and in the thirties they made most of their money from the 'cheap and cheerful' films of Deanna Durbin. The 'singing teenager' was replaced between 1940 and 1950 by the comedy team of Abbott and Costello, who in turn made way during the 1950s for Donald O'Connor and his Talking Mule, Francis.

Bud Abbott and Lou Costello made a total of thirty-six feature films and earned a total of $140 million for Universal. Their first film, *One Night in the Tropics,* was directed by A. Edward (Eddie) Sutherland, who a year earlier had directed *The Flying Deuces* with Laurel and Hardy. In fact, Laurel and Hardy were much less popular than Abbott and Costello: the reason why will always be a mystery. Comparing Stan and Oliver with Bud and Lou is like comparing a Mercedes to a Volkswagen: Abbott and Costello have far less of the charm and likeability of Laurel and Hardy.

When Abbott and Costello appeared on the doorstep of Universal Studios, they had little idea of what awaited them. They were already well-known from the radio, where they had a weekly programme consisting of old routines from their days in variety. They moved from burlesque and vaudeville through nightclubs and radio appearances to the cinema, and later on to television.

Abbot and Costello do not come across as particularly comic characters in front of the film camera. Bud is the smartly dressed, dominant character of the two, whilst Lou is a small, fat baby-faced man with desperation in his eyes. Their strength lies in their fast-moving dialogues, written by John Grant. At first, director Eddie Sutherland was not sure how to deal with Abbott and Costello, being so different to Laurel and Hardy. So all they do is stand in the middle of the studio floor and have silly discussions.

Bud: Stop smoking in here, Costello!
Lou: Who's smokin'?
Bud: You are!
Lou: What makes you think I'm smokin'?
Bud: You have a cigar in your mouth!
Lou: I've got my shoes on, but I'm not walkin'!

Their discussion of the three baseball players, Who, What and I-Don't-Know has passed into cinema history:

Bud: I say Who's on first, What's on second, I-Don't-Know's on third.
Lou: Yeah, you know the fellow's name?
Bud: Yes!

18

> Lou: Well, who's on first?
> Bud: Yes.
> Lou: I mean the fellow's name.
> Bud: Yes.
> Lou: I mean the guy playing first.
> Bud: Who!
> Lou: The fellow playing first.
> Bud: Who.
> Lou: The first baseman.
> Bud: Who.
> Lou: The guy playing first.
> Bud: Who's on first!
> Lou: Well, what are you asking me for?

And so it goes on, for a quarter of an hour.

'Who's on first?' became Abbot and Costello's catchphrase and the public heard a number of different versions of the confused discussion about the three sportsmen from their theatre and radio appearances. In the film, *The Naughty Nineties* (1945), directed by Jean Yarbrough, it appears yet again on the cinema screen, and audiences would chant it along with the actors.

Later on, in their TV shows, Bud and Lou used it again, along with large numbers of similar dialogues which they had already used in their films, on the radio and on stage. Some of their jokes were older than they were.

> Bud: You know what volts are?
> Lou: They're what?
> Bud: That's right, volts are watts.
> Lou: Well, go ahead and tell me.
> Bud: You just said it.
> Lou: I'm asking you – what are volts?
> Bud: That's right – watts are volts!
> Lou: What are you askin' *me* for?

From *Who Done It?* (1944)

Another example of typical Abbot and Costello humour:

> Bud: Suppose you were forty and you were engaged to a girl who was ten.
> Lou: O boy, this is gonna be a pip!
> Bud: Never mind. Now, you're four times older than that little girl. So you wait twenty more years. The little girl is thirty and you're sixty. Now you're only twice as old as that girl. The question is, how long do you have to wait before you and the little girl are the same age?

Feeble stuff? Possibly. But Abbot and Costello do have the ability to carry off this kind of script both on stage and screen. Straight-faced,

Bud Abbott can persuade his naive friend that he is standing not beside him, but somewhere else.

    Lou: Are you in St Louis?
    Bud: No.
    Lou: Are you in Chicago?
    Bud: Of course not!
    Lou: Well, if you're not in St Louis and you're not in Chicago, you must be somewhere else.
    Bud: Eh, Ye-es...
    Lou: Well then, if you're somewhere else, you're not here!

The idea of using material which has been around for a long time is nothing unusual or objectionable in comedy. The fact is that for centuries people have laughed at the same kind of jokes, and comedians have rarely consciously re-used or imitated others' work.

Abbott and Costello's films were very popular in the 1940s and still have a degree of popularity today through being shown on television. Each of them consists of a montage of their earlier routines, around which John Grant has skilfully woven a story. Every Abbott and Costello film has at least a few good dialogues, a perfectly timed interaction between the pair which is well worth watching.

Now the films are an average of forty years old, black-and-white and have a great deal of nostalgic appeal in view of the fact that Europe was at war but conditions in the United States were relatively comfortable (at least for those films made between 1940 and 1945), and they are still funny. Here were two comedians with a modicum of experience, gained in the twenties and thirties in a type of showbusiness where there were no technical aids to help them make people laugh. They were unique as a comedy duo, the last whose act was rooted in the type of entertainment found at the beginning of the century. They never received an Oscar, an Oscar nomination or any other form of award and, as is often the case, most critics were scathing about their films, but people queued around the block whenever a new Abbott and Costello film was shown.

Not that the American public read very much film criticism: least of all the fans of Abbott and Costello. They knew Bud and Lou from the radio, and that was enough for them. At their peak, between 1940 and 1950, they were better known and more popular than Laurel and Hardy, their predecessors in the genre.

Prior to 1940, Bud and Lou had appeared on radio a hundred times, in their 'Abbott and Costello Show' for ABC and NBC. From 1952 to 1954 CBS showed it on television, and it is still a popular programme which can be seen in the form of repeats on local TV stations.

William 'Bud' Abbott was born on 2 October 1895 in a tent belonging to Barnum and Bailey's Circus in Asbury Park, though some biographies state that he was born in 1898 in Coney Island. He was the

Abbott and Costello Meet Frankenstein (1948).

son of two circus artistes and formal education played little part in his early life (Lou Costello likewise) – neither of his parents ever read a book. According to biographer Leonard Maltin (an authority on the history of Hollywood), Bud Abbott was originally a racing driver, whilst Jim Mulholland, another expert on the subject, says that he never had a driving licence and never sat behind the wheel of a car. So we have been warned!

If we assume Abbott was born in 1895, he was eleven years younger than his partner. Lou Costello was born as Louis Francis Cristillo on 3 March 1906 in Paterson, New Jersey. He came from a family of poor Italian immigrants and decided at an early date that he wanted to be a film comedian, modelling himself on Charlie Chaplin. Costello knew every single shot of many of Chaplin's films and at the age of fourteen won a Charlie Chaplin lookalike contest in his home town.

In 1927 he hitch-hiked to Hollywood with a friend, Gene Coogan, and got a job as an upholsterer at the studios of Metro-Goldwyn-Mayer. After acting as understudy for a stuntman in a few stunts in a film directed by King Vidor, he returned to Paterson, disappointed, a year later. The one thing he realized at this stage was how much more he had to learn. On the way home, he spent his last few cents on a cup of coffee in a restaurant in St Joseph, Missouri. This was in 1930, at a time when anyone with a job in America was both able and fortunate. In St

Abbott and Costello Meet The Keystone Cops (1955), with Lynn Bari in the plane and Fred Clark with the beret.

Joseph, he saw an advertisement in a shop window: 'Dutch Comic wanted. Inquire at the Lyceum Theater.' At this time, 'Dutch' was often used to mean a stiff, formal German type with a moustache rather than specifically someone from the polders.

If you are hungry enough, you will imitate anybody's accent, and Lou Cristillo was taken on. He immediately changed his name to Costello, following the example of his brother Pat, a saxophone player.

Lou Costello learned fast, with Hollywood always at the back of his mind. A year later he was taken on by the Orpheum Theater in New York, where Bud Abbott was also on the programme. Lou Costello formed a comedy duo with Joe Lyons, whilst Bud Abbott was the straight man for Harry Evanson. Abbott and Costello both kept a close eye on each other's acts from the wings and eventually Lou suggested to Bud that they work together. Bud agreed, not without some hesitation. He was the feeder of lines to several famous comedians. In professional circles the feeder, provided he is good, is regarded as being more important than the comedian himself. The feeder gives cues to the comedian of the duo and it is he who helps the comedian to shine and shapes the situation so as to be as funny as possible. This is why, from its debut in 1937, the new comedy team was called Abbott and Costello, with the name of Bud Abbott, the straight man, coming first. Abbott was also slightly older than Costello and had been in the buiness for longer.

For a few years, Abbott and Costello toured with a travelling burlesque company doing an act called 'Life Begins at Minsky's'. This was an excellent training ground for Costello, especially with a mentor as experienced as Abbott. In 1938 they were asked to do some work for radio, and they jumped at the chance. There, Bud and Lou met Johnny Grant, who was to become their gag-writer on a permanent basis. Grant reworked a lot of Bud Abbott's existing material, which consisted of a collection of word games on the lines of 'Who's on first?'. Edward Sherman became their manager, confidant and friend.

Bud Abbott and Lou Costello were a very distinctive pair in cinema history. Although they were active in films for fifteen years and making almost weekly appearances in the radio studios at the same time, they never actually got away from being an old-fashioned variety act and were constantly being driven back and forth to the studios of Universal, ABC and NBC when really it was theatre dressing-rooms they were most used to.

Bud Abbott had been appearing for years with his brother Harry as the Abbott Brothers, and produced show programmes in the National Theater in Detroit, where he acquired an encyclopaedic knowledge of almost every American burlesque, vaudeville and variety act. This production work ended in 1918 when he married showgirl Jenny Mae Pratt and worked towards becoming the 'number one straight man'. The Abbotts adopted two children, Bud Junior (1944) and Rae Victoria (1949).

In 1950 Jenny Mae Pratt (whose stage name was Betty Smith) and Bud Abbott had their marriage re-solemnized by Rabbi Samuel Harris.

Good singers, bad actresses: the Andrews sisters, Maxen, Patty and La Verne, who appeared in three 1941 Abbott and Costello films, *Buck Privates, In the Navy* and *Hold That Ghost*.

Bud was Jewish, whilst Lou was a strict Catholic.

In 1934, Lou Costello married Anne Battler, a Scottish girl who had come to America at the age of eleven. Anne was a chorus girl, but gave up the theatre when she married Costello. The couple had four children: Patricia (Paddy, 1937), Carole Lou (1939), Louis Francis (Butch, 1942) and finally Christina (Chris, 1949).

The relationship between Bud Abbott and Lou Costello was often just as amusing as their films. Bud was an excessive drinker and suffered from epilepsy. On occasions when he had a fit whilst working in the radio, film or TV studio or when appearing live, Costello knew exactly what to do: he would hit Bud on the solar plexus in a certain way and Bud's convulsions would stop as if by magic. There may be no medical explanation for this, but it appears to have worked in Bud's case.

Lou did not often drink, but his handicap was a tendency to kleptomania. He often stole props from Universal Studios. Once he helped himself to an antique clock, used in a scene in *Abbott and Costello Meet Frankenstein* (1948) and took it home, even though it was supposed to appear on the mantlepiece in Dracula's castle in the following day's filming. Nor were Universal the only victims of this tendency. When Abbott and Costello were loaned to Metro-Goldwyn-Mayer to appear in *Lost in a Harem*, at the height of their fame in 1944, Lou helped himself to cushions and rugs and filled his car with them. Furniture, accessories, even canoes: Lou had a use for all of them! Nobody dared raise their voice in complaint, for Abbott and Costello were making a lot of money for a lot of people. When Robert Arthur, the producer of *Frankenstein,* asked Lou Costello if he would replace the purloined clock so that the crew could finish the scene, telling him he was welcome to the clock when filming was over, Lou said seriously, 'OK, will you put that in writing?' The pair also shared a passion for gambling when they were not working, a passion which was indulged to excess with their fellow artistes whenever they made a theatre appearance after Bud Abbott introduced Lou Costello to the art of playing cards. At Universal, they demanded a luxury caravan fitted with every comfort known to man, and would retreat into it at four o'clock every afternoon, on the grounds that 'Nothing's funny after four o'clock!', to gamble under Bud's expert guidance. Chris Costello, Lou's youngest daughter, was to say in 1980 in an interview with Raymond Strait: 'God knows my father was a gambler!'

So obsessed were they with this pastime that the studio crew sometimes had to carry them, chairs and all, out of the caravan and onto the set because they refused to start filming. They would never do more than one take; when it came to re-filming scenes they wanted nothing to do with it, since it meant less time to play cards.

The pair went on to star in a succession of B-movies, filmed in three weeks and ready for distribution in four, with ready-made opening and closing credits for distribution throughout the world. Bud and Lou became a valuable commodity. If Bud bought an extravagantly spacious country house, Lou would buy an even bigger one. If Bud had a swimming pool installed, Lou would have one twice as big built in his garden. On 4 November 1943, his year-old son, Butch, fell into the pool and drowned. At the time, Lou was working in the studios and was taken home by his manager, Edward Sherman. Lou Costello had worshipped his little son and never got over the tragedy. He continually accused his wife Anne of not having kept a close enough eye on him (she had been indoors on the telephone when the accident happened). The same evening, Lou Costello arrived in NBC's studios to record a live radio broadcast with Bud Abbott, and Lana Turner as the guest star. The announcer, Ken Niles, said 'And now, the Abbott and Costello programme for Camel cigarettes!' The orchestra, under Leith Stevens, struck up a tune and as the music played Lou said to Bud, 'Let's just do the best goddamn show we've ever done!' Then he yelled the introduction to the show, which was always the same: 'H-e-e-e-e-y, Abbott!'

Showbusiness is a strange affair. The show must go on: this is an unbreakable rule, no matter what may befall. It was especially true during the war, when a funny performance still had to be given, no matter how tragic events might have been outside the theatre.

As a memorial to his only son, Lou Costello carried out a number of live appearances with Bud Abbott around the country, and raised a huge sum of money. This was used to found the Lou Costello Junior Youth Foundation in Los Angeles. Several years later the financial burden of maintaining it became too much for him, and he handed it over to the City of Los Angeles, where it is still functioning today looking after young people.

After twenty-one years of working together, the comedy duo of Abbott and Costello came to a sudden end in July 1957. Bud's illness and predilection for drink made it impossible to go on. The pair often quarrelled and for long periods of time were not on speaking terms. Furthermore, demand for Abbott and Costello was on the wane, and Universal was taking on new flagship acts such as the series based on Francis, the Talking Mule. It had been Lou Costello who was initially so insistent about the two of them setting up a comedy team; likewise, it was he who ended the partnership. Their last film together was *Dance With Me, Henry,* made in 1956 by United Artists, a company which Lou's earlier idol, Charlie Chaplin, had co-founded.

The small, corpulent Lou Costello was buried on 7 March 1959, four days after his fifty-third birthday, in Calvary Cemetery in Los Angeles, next to his son Butch. He had had a heart attack a few weeks previously and died in the Doctors Hospital in Beverly Hills. Less than a year later, his wife Anne also died. When she lost Lou, she took to drink, unable to live without 'my baby'. The three children (Paddy, then 23, Carole, 20, and Chris, 12) were left with scarcely a cent between them. Lou's youngest daughter, who had taken Butch's place as the apple of Lou's eye, was entrusted to the care of Lou's brother, Pat Costello, and his wife Mary. When Lou Costello died, extracts from the 'This Is Your Life' programme made about him on 21 November 1956

The 'Abbott and Costello' cartoon series began in 1966, and was made by Bill Hanna and Joe Barbera, also responsible for shows such as 'Tom and Jerry' and 'The Flintstones'.

were shown on TV. 'Funmaker Lou Costello dies of a heart attack', said the news headlines. Bud Abbott was one of the pallbearers at the funeral, but he was so drunk he was leaning on the coffin rather than holding it up.

Bud Abbott outlived his partner by fifteen years. He breathed his last on 24 April 1974 at the Country Hospital in Hollywood, his stay financed by the Motion Picture Relief Fund because he also had nothing left of the millions of dollars he had earned during his career. A cerebral haemorrhage had left him paralysed down one side in 1968. He last worked in 1960 as straight man for Candy Candido, a comedian not unlike Jimmy Durante who attempted to take over the role of Lou Costello in the act. 'Abbott and Candido' appeared in nightclubs and large hotels. Whilst flying to Chicago, Bud suffered a severe epileptic fit. Lou would have known how to deal with it, but Candido did not know about thumping him on the stomach. Abbott never recovered and the Abbott and Candido duo lasted barely a year.

Bud Abbott reached the age of seventy-eight, and Lou Costello fifty-three. Were they an underestimated comedy team? Impossible to say, but these were two people who lived like children who suddenly find themselves in a sweetshop with a hundred-dollar bill when they have never been able to afford chocolate before. Bud and Lou were two outsized children who just wanted to enjoy life. They were conned by corrupt and bad managers (Ed Sherman). They gambled and squandered millions themselves. Their lives were wealthy, but all they left behind was a collection of wonderful comedy films.

Their friends and relatives had to sell everything to pay Bud and Lou's creditors, not least because the Internal Revenue caught up with them towards the end of their lives.

If the duo turned up today in a Woody Allen film, we would be hard put to laugh at them. This is the difference between now and 1894: people don't find it funny when someone sneezes any more.

2
Harold Lloyd: Everyone's favourite son-in-law

Harold Lloyd has rejoiced in any number of nicknames since the early 1920s. The Americans called him 'Everyman', the French '*Lui*' and the Germans '*Er*'. While Charlie Chaplin was being given such poetic epithets as 'the balletic tramp' and Buster Keaton was 'the saintly acrobat', Harold Lloyd had to make do with being described as 'that glasses character'. And although he is nearly always called Harold in his films, he usually has a different surname. There is one exception, *Safety Last* (1923), where the hero clambering along the outside of a skyscraper is called Harold Lloyd. Elsewhere he is Harold Meadows (*Girl Shy,* 1924), Harold Lamb (*The Freshman,* 1925), Harold Bledsoe (*Welcome Danger,* 1929), or Harold Horne (*Feet First,* 1930).

Harold Lloyd portrays an everyday American young man, of the up-and-coming variety. His clothes are immaculate, at least compared with the crumpled, tattered suits that other film comedians were wearing at the time. His straw hat, his then fashionable horn-rimmed glasses and the hair cut to show his ears; all these were part of the image of the man of indestructible optimism, the cheerful little man in the suit. He had no inhibitions, always going where he pleased and doing what he pleased, taking risks that none of his fellow humans would ever dream of. Despite his lack of concern for what other people think of him, he is endlessly patient and helpful as he embarks on his incredible adventures.

The surprising thing about Harold Lloyd as a comedian is that, despite his image of the timid office clerk, his films are full of the most spectacular stunts. In *High and Dizzy* (1920), *Never Weaken* (1921), *Safety Last* (1923) and *Feet First* (1930), he carries out breathtakingly daredevil climbs across girders and half-built office blocks to earn his title 'King of Daredevil Comedy'. Audiences did not know whether to tremble with fear or yell with laughter when films like these were shown. Such scenes have lost none of their appeal even now: compared to Harold Lloyd, Spiderman is a model of caution, and reviewers have called him 'The Human Fly'. There is an inescapable fascination in seeing the shy office junior desperately clutching at the hands of a clock on the side of a building a hundred feet above terra firma or balancing on a window frame or the eaves of a building with the traffic hurrying back and forth far below him.

Tradition has it that Harold Lloyd carried out these stunts himself because as a former amateur boxer and athlete he could make a better job of such dangerous tasks than the stand-ins who might have done it for him. He never had a single accident during any of these episodes, be it crawling up the side of a building or clutching onto the top of a moving tram (*Girl Shy,* 1924). Ironically, though, like an off-duty fighter pilot falling off his bicycle, Lloyd did have one accident whilst having a publicity photograph taken in the studio during a break from the making of *Haunted Spooks* (1920). On 24 August 1919, a photographer decided that it would be good if Lloyd lit a cigarette using a round, black fake 'bomb'. The prop-man gave him the bomb, with its fuse burning and held it to his face to light the cigarette. The stills man took a photograph, and then another, and then another. Then the bomb exploded very realistically. Harold Lloyd lost the thumb and index finger of his right hand (hence the fact that he wears gloves in all his subsequent films), his face was injured and his sight was impaired for months afterwards.

The public never noticed his injuries, and even on close examination it is impossible to see that he had artificial fingers or felt in any way

Left: 'College Boy' Harold
Lloyd. Right: Bebe Daniels
(1901-71), Lloyd's first
leading lady.

handicapped by the injuries. His use of his hands is perfectly natural and
he makes no attempt to keep his right hand out of frame.

Harold Lloyd made 165 shorts, 11 'silent' full-length feature films
(though the pianist and announcer between them used to make more
noise than a talking film) and 7 features with sound. More than half his
short films no longer exist, at least not in the United States. The films
were made on nitrate, which has a comparatively short life, and a fire in
Lloyd's film vault in 1934 destroyed a quarter of his work. There are
undoubtedly copies of some of the missing films in film collections and
museums in Europe. Since 1975, multi-media giant Time Life has been
bringing out many 'patched-up' Harold Lloyd films for circulation in
independent cinemas, universities and eventually for television. For this
reason, Harold Lloyd's films have enjoyed something of a renaissance,
with a great deal more public showings than had hitherto been the case.
Lloyd being an extravagantly rich man who right up till the end of his
life preferred to provide for the future than look back at the past, few of
his films were shown in 'Comedy Capers'-type TV programmes during
the fifties and sixties. Lloyd distributed his own films in the United
States and was opposed to this and, given the money that he made from
the re-issues, there was no need for him to do so. Not until 1962 did he
make his own compilation, *Harold Lloyd's World of Comedy*, a superb
montage of the best of *Safety Last, The Freshman, Hot Water, Why
Worry, Girl Shy, Professor Beware, Movie Crazy* and *Feet First*. When
he introduced the film at the 1962 Cannes Film Festival he received a
long standing ovation from journalists and fellow film-makers after the

Harry Langdon (left).

press showing. Ten years before, he received an Oscar, with the accolade: 'Harold Lloyd: a Master Comedian and a Good Citizen'. *Harold Lloyd's World of Comedy* marked a revival of interest in his films amongst the public, not least for the nostalgia value of the Model T Fords, trams, buses, broad avenues and magnificent buildings which they portrayed in such profusion. The public particularly enjoyed renewing its acquaintance with Harold, the 'All-American Boy' who embodied the optimistic spirit of the New World. America was experiencing renewed pleasure in films with happy endings, where the heroes and heroines could look forward to material comfort and well-being.

The compilation, which Lloyd refused to allow anyone else to make for him, was shown in two cinemas off London's Leicester Square. A reviewer from the *Daily Mail* noted that once again a new generation of cinemagoers was coming out of the cinema with tears rolling down its face from having laughed so much. In America, people queued for hours to see *Harold Lloyd's World of Comedy*.

In his films, Harold Lloyd appears as a self-made man, a small-town boy with great ambitions who manages to keep his bespectacled head above water in the Big City. In fact, the real star was very like the fictional character; not for nothing did the Oscar citation call him a 'Good Citizen', a title which could not be applied to Charlie Chaplin at this stage. Chaplin had to wait slightly longer for his Academy Award.

Harold Clayton Lloyd was born on 20 April 1893 in the small hamlet of Burchard, Nebraska. His father was a photographer and billiard-hall owner, James Darsie Lloyd. He received no education whatsoever. In 1912 he made his cinema début as an Indian with the Edison Company. He went on to play in Mack Sennett comedies until in 1914 he met and

The strong resemblance between Harold Lloyd and King Baudouin of Belgium led some people to suggest it was actually Lloyd portrayed on the stamps.

befriended a fellow actor, Hal E. Roach. Roach was then starting his own business, Rolin Film Company. Rolin's first comedy quartet consisted of Harold Lloyd as the comedian Willie Work, sidekick Snub Pollard, leading lady Bebe Daniels and 'heavy' Bud Jamison.

The one-act Willie Work films were not a success and did not sell. The team achieved better results with the hundred or so Lonesome Luke comedies, where Lloyd borrowed somewhat from the Chaplinesque figure of the tramp as hero. The Lonesome Luke films were particularly popular from 1916 to 1918, not least because fifteen-year-old actress Bebe Daniels portrayed an adult woman with dark eyes and a sensual body. Bebe Daniels was the female screen idol of the time. When she left Rolin to work for Cecil B. De Mille at Paramount, this marked the demise of the somewhat unoriginal figure of Lonesome Luke. Some sources say that Lloyd dropped the character on the advice of Hal Roach; others that he himself had had enough of Luke and wanted to embark on something rather more original.

It was at this point that the Everyman figure was introduced by Lloyd and Roach: the straw hat, owlish glasses, three-piece suit or white trousers and blazer and a mode of behaviour to match the clothing. It represented quite a contrast with other comedians who were around at the time, but they took the risk and it paid off. The pair moved gradually from making shorts to full-length features, again something of a risk as the comedy studios were not at home with long films.

In 1923, the two film-makers parted amicably and went their separate ways in show business. Lloyd wanted to continue producing his own films and set up the Harold Lloyd Corporation to do so. His father was one of the directors, his uncle William Frazer the manager of the business, whilst John L. Murphy moved from Rolin to become chief producer. Lloyd distributed his own films within the United States, though abroad they were distributed by Paramount. This was a very satisfactory division of labour from Lloyd's point of view, and it meant that he made very much more from his films than ever Harry Langdon, Buster Keaton or Laurel and Hardy did.

On 10 February 1923 Harold Lloyd married his co-star in many of his films, Mildred Davis. They stayed together until Mildred died of a heart attack on 18 August 1969. Lloyd himself died of cancer at the age of seventy-seven, on 8 March 1971. His first leading lady (and, according to the press of the day, his first great love), Bebe Daniels, died in London only eight days after Lloyd.

Duke Lloyd, Harold's only son, who was born in January 1931, died of a stroke three months after his father. Lloyd's daughter Gloria (born on 22 May 1924) was forced to go to a clinic in Switzerland after marital troubles made her a manic depressive. In 1930 Harold and Mildred adopted a five-year-old daughter, Peggy, as a companion for Gloria. When Lloyd died, he left Gloria and Peggy and his grand-daughter Suzanne (Gloria's daughter) $5 million between them. Greenacres, his huge home at 1225 Benedict Canyon Drive in Beverly Hills, which had

forty rooms, two lifts, a garden with twelve fountains, an Olympic-sized swimming pool, tennis courts and a golf course, a boating lake, and a tiny playhouse for the two girls complete with gas and electricity, was given to the Harold Lloyd Foundation and now serves as the Hollywood Museum and a place of pilgrimage for Harold Lloyd fans.

Harold and Mildred Lloyd moved into the $2 million property in 1928. It took thirty people to look after the home, plus two permanent projectionists employed to run Lloyd's in-house cinema, where a hundred luxurious seats were used to entertain Lloyd's colleagues and friends.

Lloyd loved parties, and his were the talk of Hollywood and the surrounding area. A house party at Greenacres would normally begin at lunchtime on a Friday and go on until Monday evening. Whenever he was at home, he liked to be surrounded by people. Just before she died, Mildred Lloyd told journalist Hedda Hopper that she found the house too large and unfriendly, especially when the children were not there. The lift was about all she liked: 'It was the only cosy place in the house!' Many film and TV recordings have taken place at Greenacres in more recent years, including 'Columbo' and 'Cannon'. Its gardens are also used for fashion shows and as an exotic setting for videos and advertisements.

American film stars of the thirties and forties often lived like kings and queens: it was their entitlement, because they had worked for it. This was what the public expected and the 'victims' were more than happy with their lot. Examples of their almost unbelievable wealth can be found in almost any book about Hollywood.

The period of the silent film was dominated by Charlie Chaplin, Buster Keaton, Harold Lloyd and Harry Langdon. Harry (Baby Face) Langdon is a passive comedian, a helpless clown caught up in the raging torrent of life. Frank Capra, who for a while was his director, producer and adviser, joined him in making the three best feature films he starred in: *Tramp, Tramp, Tramp* (1926), *The Strong Man* (1927) and *Long Pants* (1927). Frank Capra very quickly saw that Langdon was a genius at pantomime acting with a great deal of talent for making films, but after these three superb features, made for First National Pictures (later Warner Bros) he decided that he no longer wanted to make films with Capra, preferring instead to direct his own films. He wandered from one studio to another and made a number of cheap one- and two-reelers, all fast-moving comedies with a great deal of falling over and throwing things around. In his biography, *The Name Above the Title*,

Never Weaken (1921), Harold Lloyd's second 'daredevil comedy'.

Frank Capra says of his break-up with Harry Langdon: 'I left – and I could have cried. That great, great artist – whose art was the very essence of slow, slow pantomime – was being hollered at to go faster!'

Compared to Harry Langdon, Harold Lloyd was very much a doer who liked to be in command of whatever he did. Even in his everyday life he was more businesslike than Langdon. At the pinnacle of their success, the order of popularity was Chaplin, Keaton, Lloyd and Langdon. This was borne out in the polls carried out by the *Motion Pictures Herald,* which published an annual Top Ten. From my own experience, it would seem that nowadays Harold Lloyd would come top of the order of popularity, above even Charlie Chaplin. His silent films are especially popular, most notably *Safety Last* (1923), with its famous clock scene. Likewise the 1930 sound film, *Feet First,* with Lloyd playing a shoe salesman, Harold Horne, and with a *tour de force* from Hollywood's best-known drunkard (though the actor himself never touched a drop), Arthur Housman, has been shown on television many times, always with great success.

In 1938, Harold Lloyd produced his last feature film, *Professor Beware.* For reasons which are not entirely clear, Harold Lloyd Films went on to produce films for RKO which Lloyd himself did not act in. This was a very surprising step for him to take, probably taken for reasons personal to Lloyd himself. He went on to produce films such as *A Girl, A Guy and A Cop* (1941) and *My Favourite Spy* (1942).

It was not until 1946 that writer and director Preston Sturges managed to persuade him to appear before the camera again and act in a

Harold Lloyd (left) and Hal E. Roach in 1922.

Professor Beware (1938), an off-screen shot with a group of young extras.

comedy, *The Sin of Harold Diddlebock*. The film begins with the heroic rugby match from *The Freshman* (1924), in which Harold emerges as a great hero. There is a jump in time to 1945, and Harold is sitting at the same desk as in *The Freshman*: he is older, but no wiser.

The film was brought out by United Artists at the end of 1946, but was something of a failure. In January 1947, Cathleen Dash wrote in the *Culver City Star News*: 'Only Harold Lloyd seems to be enjoying himself in the Preston Sturges comedy, *The Sin of Harold Diddlebock*!'. Harold's adventures twenty years after his rugby triumph in *The Freshman* failed to grasp the public imagination. In 1950, RKO brought out a shortened version of the film, entitled *Mad Wednesday*, but this was no more of a success.

A year before his death, in February 1970, Harold Lloyd was introducing some of his films to a group of university students in New York. The participants in this workshop were young, and some of them had never seen any of his films before. Apart from Harold Lloyd's own achievements in making the films, the students were also impressed by the brilliant camerawork of Walter Lundin. He played a very important part in the rooftop scenes, and Harold Lloyd was keen to emphasize the importance of the cameraman. When one student asked him whether he had ever been afraid whilst risking his life to make these scenes, Harold Lloyd said, almost shyly, 'No, I always liked it, I always liked it...'

3

The Marx Brothers: Brothers before the Warners

There were five Marx brothers, all sons of the Jewish tailor Samuel Marx from New York City, who migrated to the United States from Alsace, and his wife Minna Schoenberg, the daughter of a magician. The brothers were Chico (1886-1961, real name Leonard Marx), Harpo (1888-1964, Adolph, later Arthur Marx), Groucho (1890-1977, Julius Henry Marx), Gummo (Milton Marx, 1893-1977)

and Zeppo (1901-79, Herbert Marx).

The Brothers had already successfully established themselves in vaudeville when they embarked on their cinematic career (minus Gummo) in 1929. In the early twenties Groucho, Harpo, Chico and Zeppo had made their own film with two other friends, Al Posen and Max Lippman, for $6000. Filmed in Fort Lee, New Jersey, and a small Tenth Avenue studio in New York, and variously titled 'Humoresque', 'Humorisk' and 'Humo Risk' the film was lost, and film collectors and historians have been searching for a copy for decades. When Richard J. Anobile interviewed Groucho Marx in 1971 and asked the whereabouts of the silent film, Groucho replied: 'I haven't the faintest idea. Fifty years ago! You expect me to remember what I did fifty years ago? Quick, let's go on.'

When the Marx Brothers left the stage, they were already mature comedians, but they went on to make five films as a foursome. Then followed nine films with Groucho, Harpo and Chico, five with Groucho alone and two with solo performances by Harpo. The best known are the thirteen films they made from 1929 to 1949, beginning with *The Cocoanuts* and ending with *Love Happy*.

The films never enjoyed the huge success with mainstream cinema audiences in Europe that they did in the United States. In the thirties and forties the Marx Brothers were too eccentric for many Europeans,

A Night at the Opera (1935): Harpo Marx.

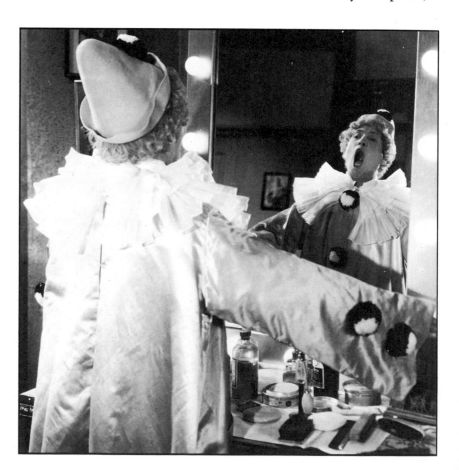

their humour too aggressive. Groucho fired high-speed insults at everyone and everything in sight and the gags reached hitherto undreamed-of levels of absurdity. It is sometimes an effort to keep up with Groucho with his huge fake moustache, equally huge Havana cigar and extraordinary gait. Add to the the difficulty of translating the jokes into any language other than English, and you have a formidable combination. Many European translators were floored by examples such as Groucho saying 'I would buy you a parachute if I thought it wouldn't open' and Chico replying 'I already got a pair of shoes!'

In his films, Groucho Marx surveys the world slyly through his intellectual-looking glasses. He plays with the cinema audience, throwing ambiguous, knowing glances at them from the screen, and constantly moves around with a long, shuffling gait as though about to fall over. He is like a caricature of an American gentleman, retailing an embellished version of the truth, a fast-talking crooked lawyer. He has enormous destructive power as well: an ability to demolish his opponents psychologically which outshines anything that Lenny Bruce or Bob Hope could ever manage. Groucho is everyone's boss; no one else gets a look in, and in many ways his films are one-man shows.

Chico Marx is totally unlike Groucho. Constantly dressed in corduroy complete with distinctive hunting cap, the image is mainly that of the Italian immigrant having trouble with his English. He is less

Go West (1940): Groucho with fake moustache and Stetson as S. Quentin Quale, Harpo (right) as Rusty Panello and Chico Marx as Joseph Panello at the piano; the actress is Diana Woods.

of a businessman than Groucho, dealing in turn in dirty postcards, sweets and ice-cream. He is a virtuoso pianist, though, rivalling Victor Borge both in musical skill and humour. Now and then he makes an attempt at oral humour, but rarely pulls it off the way Groucho does. In *Monkey Business* (1931), for example, he says to brother Harpo: 'I'll do anything for money. I'd even kill someone for money. Even you! No, you're my friend, I'd kill you for free!' And to Groucho: 'I haven't eaten for three days: not yesterday, not today, and not tomorrow!' Stan Laurel says the same thing to his benefactor Mary Carr in *One Good Turn*, also from 1931.

Brother No. 3, Harpo Marx, never opens his mouth in any of the films; his forte is whistling. He communicates using his harp and also a walking stick with a hooter mounted on top, which is always by his side. He also 'talks' using gestures and a wide variety of wind instruments. The oversized jackets he wears come in useful to support his incurable habit of stealing things; he is a kind of magical clown. With his curly hair and huge, innocent child's eyes, he often looks like the most touching of the three brothers. But appearances can be deceptive: he is a genius at picking pockets, and even manages on one occasion to relieve Groucho of half his false teeth. He is totally omnivorous: he devours a telephone with relish, drinks ink, and likes flowers mainly because they taste so nice. Buttons off people's uniforms are a particular delicacy, particularly if they are shiny ones. As if that was not enough, he is an inveterate womanizer and has the irritating habit, when a hand is extended to him in greeting, of hooking his right knee over the person's arm, faster than the eye can see, inducing a wide range of hilarious expressions on the faces of his victims.

In 1948, United Artists were making the Marx Brothers film *A Night in Casablanca*, a parody of the 1942 Bogart classic, *Casablanca*. They offered Harpo $50,000 if he would shout one word in the film: 'Murder!' This would have meant they could advertise the film with the slogan 'Harpo Speaks!' The Brothers refused, and the gimmick of the stoically silent Harpo remained intact. This was not due to his being unable to speak, but apparently he stopped learning any new words when he was a child. None the less, with the help of Rowland Barber he later wrote a 650-page autobiography called *Harpo Speaks!* (Bernard Geis Associates, New York, 1961).

Groucho was inevitably the subject of much of the material written by and about the Marx Brothers. The sayings of the 'King of the Insult' have been published in book form, and books he wrote himself include *Groucho and Me* (Bernard Geis Associates, New York, 1959), *Memoirs of a Mangy Lover* (Manor Books, 1963/4) and *The Groucho Letters* (Simon and Schuster, 1967). Every page of these books contains brilliantly quotable lines.

Until the end of his life, Groucho was a sharp-witted man who took a great deal of pleasure in putting fellow humans in their place. From 5 October 1950 to 21 September 1961, NBC gave him the chance to insult studio guests in front of an audience of millions in the quiz show,

'At the Circus', 1939,
Groucho and Chico Marx.

'You Bet Your Life', which Groucho presented. His sarcastic humour struck a chord with the viewing public and the programme was a great success. Even now, extracts are occasionally shown on TV under the title 'The Best of Groucho'. When interviewing one woman for the show, Groucho asked a mother of thirteen why she had so many children. 'I love my husband,' replied the woman. Said Groucho: 'And I love my cigar, but I do take it out now and then!' Another guest told him that the waiter in Groucho's favourite restaurant had died that morning. Unmoved, Groucho replied: 'Oh yes? So God finally managed to catch his eye?'

Groucho Marx married three times. None of his wives (Ruth, Kay and Eden) could live with his personality, and all eventually turned to drink. In 1970, when Groucho was eighty, twenty-nine-year-old secretary Erin Fleming came into his life and they became friends. When journalists asked him about the difference in their ages, he said 'A man is as old as the woman he feels!', and insisted 'My relationship with Erin is purely physical!' Of the origins of the Marx Brothers he said: 'The Marx Brothers have always been brothers. In fact, we were brothers before the Warners!' Here he was alluding to Harry, Albert, Sam and Jack Warner, who set up the Warner Brothers Company in 1923 and were usually referred to in the film industry as The Brothers.

Although the part played by Chico, Harpo and Zeppo in the films of the Marx Brothers was an important one, many fans regarded the films first and foremost as a vehicle for Groucho. After about 1970, his films became more popular than they had ever been before. Although most of the comedians mentioned in this book had nothing directly to do with television, when it was invented and later when video recorders became widespread the films were suddenly freely available to everyone. Whether the Performing Rights associations like it or not, the time is now fast approaching when anyone will be able to buy the complete works of any given director, actor or actress in simple and convenient form.

Monkey Business (1931): Groucho on the deck of the boat he has stowed away on.

Groucho Marx made the long progression from vaudeville and musicals through film to television, and he always maintained that television would enable a new generation to see and appreciate the Marx Brothers' films. And he was right: they are still engrained in our culture. Pop group Queen, for example, released an LP in November 1975 entitled 'A Night at the Opera', named after the Marx Brothers film made in 1935, and a year later made 'A Day at the Races', from the 1937 film of the same name. Groucho retaliated for the misappropriation of his film titles by publicly declaring that he was in the process of making a film called 'The Rolling Stones Story'. And now, in the late 1980s, a film like *The Cocoanuts*, made in 1929, still has a modern, fresh feel to it after over fifty years.

The writers of the Marx Brothers' scripts were Morrie Ryskind (b. 1895), Bert Kalmar (1884-1947), Sidney Joseph Perelman (1904-1979) and George S. Kaufman (1889-1961). All were masters of the art of wordplay, a mastery they shared with H. M. Walker (1887-1939), who wrote for comedians such as Laurel and Hardy. Kaufman said of the Brothers in an undated interview: 'The Marx Brothers are comedians, but actually putting up with them – that's no joke!' Nor did they often pay much attention to scripts: they ad-libbed so often that George Kaufman once interrupted a rehearsal by saying, semi-seriously, 'Sorry guys, but did I just hear a sentence I actually wrote?'

It was Kaufman, too, who came up with the advice that was given to all scriptwriters working for the Brothers: 'The best thing to do is just say "Groucho comes on, Chico comes on, Harpo comes on." They'll fill in the rest themselves and the bill will get paid on time!'

The Marx Brothers got their screen names from Art Fisher, who thought up nicknames for Hollywood actors and actresses as a sideline. Their names were inspired by a daily strip cartoon in the *New York Journal* called 'Mager's Monks'. The characters in this cartoon, written by Charles A. Mager, had names reflecting their obsessions: Knocko, Sherlocko, Hamfatto and Nervo. Chico Marx got his name because of his romantic streak (he liked 'chicks'), Harpo because of his harp, Gummo because of his passion for crepe-soled shoes, Groucho because of his frequently morose expression. Zeppo is the only 'fake' name which does not actually mean anything: Herbert Marx was the youngest and most ordinary of the Brothers and Art Fisher could not see any specific traits which might have given him a nickname.

To end this chapter (though the subject of the Marx Brothers is worthy of a few hundred more pages at least), an extract from their first sound film, *The Cocoanuts*, made in 1929. Groucho Marx plays Mr Hammer, the owner of a seaside hotel. The telephone rings in reception and Groucho says: 'Hello? Yes? Ice water in 318? Is that so? Where'd you get it? Oh, you want some? Oh, that's different. Have you got any ice? No, I haven't. This is Cocoanut Beach – no snow, no ice. Get some onions. That will make your *eyes water*. (Silence) What? (Silence) You too!'

Like a good book, a good film never grows old.

4

George Formby: A young man and a ukelele

George Formby did a lot for Brylcreem sales in Britain and elsewhere. With his slicked-down, neatly cut hair and friendly, innocent grin, he was a simple, uncomplicated type who was described as a 'Toothy ukelele music-hall entertainer'. Between 1936 and 1943 he was easily Britain's most popular film comedian, his straightforward films packing them in at the local Odeon cinema.

Formby was very much a Northerner: he was born in Wigan on 26 May 1904 as George Booth. At the time, there was a certain amount of inbuilt resistance to comedians with Lancashire accents; Southerners liked to pretend they could not understand a Northern accent, and George Formby never shook off his. This was also the reason why his films never gained popularity in the United States; Sir Michael Balcon (1896-1977), a producer at the Ealing Studios where George Formby made eleven of his films, did put together a 'trade show' consisting of highlights from Formby's films in an attempt to interest the American market in 'the guy with the banjulele', but his eventual verdict was 'You couldn't sell in the United States a Lancashire accent! *[sic]*' It is difficult to disagree with his statement, though Stan Laurel never found himself handicapped by his Northern English accent.

In early twentieth-century America, most people with a little perseverance had a chance to make the transition from the theatre or circus to cinema comedy. This was not the case in Britain, and it was rare for an actor, actress, producer or director to make it to the big time on the screen. The number of people out of work in show business at any one time was enormous, and competition was fierce. Those people who did succeed in British cinema comedy usually came from the music hall, and later from the radio. Famous examples included Gracie Fields (1898-1979; one of her best-known films was *Sally in our Alley),* Max Miller (1895-1963) and Will Fyffe (1885-1947, a Scottish music-hall comedian who won national fame with his song 'I belong to Glasgow'). The list of theatre and cinema comedians is endless, and there was no shortage of comedy teams in the late twenties and thirties: Walls and Lynn, Lucan and MacShane, Askey and Murdoch, Hulbert and Courtneidge, Elsie and Doris Waters and dozens of others. It is

It's in the Air (1938), the best known Formby comedy, with George as the native RAF recruit, plus Polly Ward (b.1908) and Jack Hobbs (1893-1968).

therefore almost a miracle that George Formby managed such a runaway success in the cinema against such competition.

George made his début at the age of ten in a short, low-budget silent film made by a director who was later to be one of the pioneers of Ealing, Will Barker. The film was called *By the Shortest of Heads* (1914). Twenty years later, in 1934, Formby played alongside his wife Beryl in a garage in Albany Street, London, which had been converted into a studio: the film was *Boots Boots.* Despite its low budget, the film was an immediate success in the North, where George had earned some recognition already as a theatre entertainer and up-and-coming record artist. He then made a second film, *Off the Dole,* which consolidated his reputation in Northern England and landed him a contract with Ealing Studios in West London.

George Formby's first two Ealing films, *No Limit* (1935) and *Keep Your Seats Please* (1936) were directed by the comedian Monty Banks (1897-1950), who had emigrated from Italy to America in 1914 as Mario Bianchi and worked with comedians such as Roscoe 'Fatty' Arbuckle. In 1928 Monty Banks moved to England, married the comedienne Gracie Fields and directed the two Formby films. Later, back in America, Banks was to direct such films as *Great Guns* with Stan Laurel and Oliver Hardy.

George's leading lady in *No Limit* and *Keep Your Seats Please* was the review actress and dancer, Florence Desmond ('the greatest Lancashire Lass of them all!'), whose undeniable sex appeal strengthened the slightly effete image of George. Other attractive co-stars included Kay Walsh, Googie Withers and Phyllis Calvert.

Monty Banks (1897-1950): director of Formby's first two Ealing comedies, *No Limit* (1935) and *Keep Your Seats Please* (1936).

The chaotic plots of George Formby's films do not bear recounting. I have not seen them all, but most of them show George as a pleasant, very serious and somewhat hard-done-by character constantly trying to Get His Girl. In some ways it is his seriousness which provides the humour in his films: his habit for example, of picking up a banjo, ukelele, guitar, mandoline or other small stringed instrument and composing a ballad to the women he loves. Like his fellow comedian and rival, Joe E. Brown, he is graced with a conspicuously immaculate set of teeth and like Joe is given to emitting cries of joy at every available opportunity: 'Ooooh Mother!'

Formby's films traditionally end with a comic chase sequence, on motorbikes, cars, aeroplanes or even on horseback. Just before the closing titles, 'The End – An Ealing Picture', George gets his girl and we see that our hero is obviously not as stupid as he looks. In *Keep Your Seats Please* a goat eats the seat of a chair which had been used to hide valuables in, a bequest to George. So George disguises the goat as a dog and takes it to hospital by bus to get an X-ray of it. George's attempts to help as the X-ray is being taken are hilarious, with something of the atmosphere of the American comedies of the time, especially when the photo reveals that all the goat has swallowed is a pair of scissors, a can opener and some buttons. But in general his films are in a class apart, bearing little comparison with their Hollywood equivalents. The type

Top: George Formby.
Bottom: Formby playing a
jockey in *Come On George*
(1939).

he portrays is always similar, whether he be a bus conductor *(Keep Your Seats Please,* 1936), a jockey in *Come on George* in 1940 (for a while Formby did actually work as a jockey), an RAF officer in *It's in the Air* (1939) or a pseudo-police officer in *Spare a Copper* (1941).

By 1942 it was apparent that as an English film comedian George Formby was unable to hold his own in the popularity stakes against America's 'jesters of the silver screen' such as Red Skelton, the Marx Brothers and Joe E. Brown. The former cornerstone of the small, but productive Ealing Studios, then owned by the BBC, was replaced by Will Hay (1888–1949) who came from Gainsborough Studios and made a few good films at Ealing.

Turned Out Nice Again (1941), directed by Marcel Vernel, was the last film George Formby made at Ealing. Ealing went on to establish itself a major reputation as a comedy studio and gradually turned to high-quality humour, with directors such as Charles Crichton (*Passport to Pimlico,* 1949; *The Lavender Hill Mob,* 1951, and *The Titfield Thunderbolt,* 1952) and Alexander Mackendrick, laid a firm foundation for a whole series of classic British film comedies. Mackendrick was responsible for such world-famous films as *Whisky Galore* (1949), *The Man in the White Suit* (1951), *Mandy* (1952), *The Maggie* (1953) and *The Lady Killers* (1955). As this was going on, Formby was producing B-movies which Ealing used in double bills with its own films.

George Formby went to work for Columbia-British, where he made six films between 1942 and 1946. None of these was anything like as funny as his Ealing comedies. His film career ended with *George in Civvy Street* (1946) and for a few years the south of England heard little more of him.

Beryl, Formby's wife, was a strong-willed woman who acted as

No Limit (1935): George wins the Isle of Man TT Race.

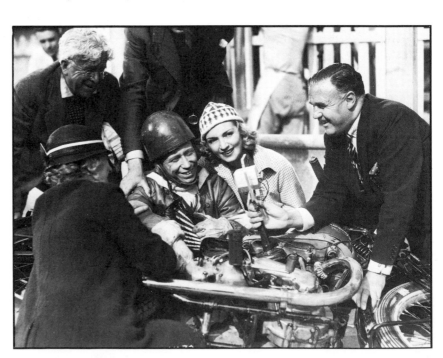

business manager and impresario for her husband. It was she who
would read the studio contracts that arrived on their doormat, adding
her own opinions. George would sign anything Beryl put in front of
him. According to the stories circulating about him in Britain (there
being little or no interest in his career from abroad), although he was
one of the ten best-paid film actors in the country, Beryl gave him only
small amounts of pocket money.

In 1951, Formby made an attempt to return to the stage, playing in
light comedies such as *Zip Goes a Million* at the Palace Theatre in
London. A year and a half later he had a minor heart attack and was
ordered to rest. In 1956 he made another attempt to return to the stage,
this time as Idle Jack in *Dick Whittington*. Although the public was on
his side, he was having serious problems in his personal life. His health
was poor, and on 24 December 1960 his wife Beryl died. The British
press was inundated with indignant letters when he announced his
intention to marry a teacher who was somewhat younger than him, Pat
Howson: the British public was disapproving. But when he told in a TV
interview how Beryl had frequently been drunk and he was at the mercy
of her fits of depression, Britain forgave him.

On 6 March 1961, a few days before the marriage, George Formby
died. He was fifty-six.

There is now a flourishing George Formby Fan Club in Britain,
with its own magazine and a large number of nostalgic members. His
black-and-white films have been brought out on video under the
auspices of the Fan Club, and selections from his 78s can be bought on
LP. In short, his work is enjoying a revival. George Formby look-alikes
are in great demand and sheet music of his songs, with a photo of him
on the cover, are selling better than ever before.

Perhaps the song he will be best remembered for is 'When I'm
Cleaning Windows' which at one stage was almost the second national
anthem. Older readers might still remember the words Formby sings as
he stands on his ladder in *Keep Your Seats Please*.

> I go window cleaning to earn an honest bob;
> For a nosey parker it's an interesting job.
>
> Now it's a job that suits me,
> A window cleaner you would be,
> If you could see what I can see
> When I'm cleaning windows.
>
> The honeymoon couples too,
> You should see them bill and coo.
> You'd be surprised at what they do
> When I'm cleaning windows.
>
> In my profession I work hard, but I'll never stop.
> I'll climb the blinking ladder till I get right to the top.

48

The blushing bride looks so divine,
The bridegroom he is doing fine.
I'd rather have his job than mine
When I'm cleaning windows.

The chambermaid sweet names I call,
It's a wonder I don't fall.
My mind's not on my work at all
When I'm cleaning windows.

I know a fellow, such a swell,
He has a thirst, that I could tell.
I've seen him drink his bath as well
When I'm cleaning windows.

In my profession I work hard, but I'll never stop.
I'll climb the blinking ladder till I get right to the top.

Pyjamas lying side by side,
Ladies' nighties I have spied.
I've often seen what goes inside
When I'm cleaning windows.

Now there's a famous talkie queen,
She looks a flapper on the screen,
She's more like eighty than eighteen
When I'm cleaning windows.

She pulls her hair all down behind,
Then pulls down her…never mind,
And after that pulls down the blind,
When I'm cleaning windows.

In my profession I work hard, but I'll never stop.
I'll climb the blinking ladder till I get right to the top.

An old maid walks around the floor,
She's so fed up, one day I'm sure
She'll drag me in and lock the door
When I'm cleaning windows.

5
Stan Laurel and Oliver Hardy: In a class of their own

From 1927 to 1950 Stan Laurel (Arthur Stanley Jefferson, 1890-1965) and Oliver Hardy (Norvell Hardy, 1892-1957) were the best-known and most popular pair of screen comedians in cinema history. Their work consisted of 81 shorts and 24 longer feature films varying in length from an hour to an hour and a half.

Stan Laurel was a product of the British music hall, having toured

Four-year-old Jacquie Lyn
with 'uncles' Stan and Oliver
in *Pack Up Your Troubles*
(1932).

England and Scotland as a boy comedian with Fred Karno's London
Comedians, one of Karno's several entertainment groups. In 1913 he
went to America for the second time, with 'The Mummingbirds', or as
it was called in the States 'A Night in an English Music Hall'. This time
he stayed.

Unlike Stan Laurel, Oliver Hardy did not come from a family of
entertainers. Originally his mother owned a hotel in Milledgeville,
Georgia, but Hardy moved into a job as manager of Milledgeville's first
cinema and then found work with the Lubin film company in
Jacksonville, Florida. At first, he worked as the 'heavy' in comedies by
Chaplin imitator Billy West, Larry Semon, Earle Williams and Jimmy
Aubrey. By the time he signed a contract with Hal Roach in 1924, he
had built himself up a successful career as a film actor, director and 'gag
man'.

A year earlier, in 1923, producer Hal Roach had signed up the red-
haired Briton, Stan Laurel, initially as a comedian and later on as a
director and scriptwriter. His first film working as a director with
Roach was *Yes, Yes, Nanette*. In 1926 the pair first appeared together in
Get 'em Young, though as separate actors, not a duo. In 1917 they had

also played separately in *Lucky Dog,* a film by Gilbert 'Broncho Billy' Anderson. Ten years later, they were playing together in *Duck Soup,* (1927), and eventually Leo McCarey, the producer and director who discovered them and turned them into a duo, had them working together in *Putting Pants on Philip* (1927), where Stan spends the time walking around in a kilt, minus underwear. In 1928, Hal Roach's

studios began the 'Laurel and Hardy Comedies' series in Culver City: This series was to continue until 1935 and began with *Should Married Men Go Home?* (1928).

Our Relations (1936), with James Finlayson as Chief Stoker of the S.S. *Periwinkle.*

In the early 1960s, Hal Roach Studios were sold and demolished. The site of the world's most famous 'fun factory' is now graced by somewhat less attractive supermarkets and car showrooms. Laurel and Hardy's last feature film was *Atoll K,* shot on location on the French Riviera during 1951 and 1952. It is not a funny film and its only real interest is the chance to see the pair appearing together one more time. The last films they made in America were in 1945; these were a good deal better than *Atoll K,* but still not as brilliant as the Hal Roach films: This is not a criticism, but merely a sad statement of fact, and it was not really Stan and Oliver's fault. When they were working with Hal Roach they enjoyed a great deal of artistic independence, and Stan Laurel in particular played a major role in deciding what the audience eventually saw, rather than simply appearing as an actor. With 20th Century-Fox, on the other hand, they disliked the bureaucratic film-factory atmosphere. However, they did the best they could and made six feature films for the company. Later, they made a further two for

Metro-Goldwyn-Mayer (*Air Raid Wardens*, 1943 and *Nothing But Trouble*, 1945).

There were many reasons which contributed to the fact that the Hal Roach films evolved a style which has remained inimitable to this day and given generation after generation of filmgoers so much pleasure. The studio at 8822 Washington Boulevard was small and friendly, and the people who earned their daily bread there formed a close-knit family. Not that there were not many distinctive personalities working in the studios: there was the self-willed Hal Roach, scriptwriting genius Hiram M. Walker (1887-1937), the erudite chief of production, Leo McCarey (1898-1969), and such great directors and cameramen as George and Jack Stevens, Ray and of course Leo McCarey, Art Lloyd, James and Charley Parrott (the latter better known as comedian Charley Chase), James W. Horne, Gordon Douglas and Fred Guiol. There was the greatly underestimated sound technician Elmer R. Raguse, editors Richard Currier and Bert Jordan, and composers T. Marvin Hatley and LeRoy Shield, to name but a few. In this warm, close-knit environment everyone worked their hardest to ensure the best possible finished product: films that would make the ordinary man or woman in the street laugh when they went to the cinema. There were no lengthy rehearsals, no market research to examine target audiences – they simply used intuition and sensitivity to decide what was and was not funny, and then made a perfect, high-quality film. This was the ideal environment for Laurel and Hardy's comic talents to develop, and they continue to give pleasure to audiences today as a result.

A major factor in their rediscovery came when John Quinn, with the help of the New York Museum of Modern Art and other organizations, made new copies of six of Laurel and Hardy's two-reelers more than fifty years after the films were first made. These were shown under the title *The Return of Laurel and Hardy* in two New York cinemas, with live music. Half a century after their première, people queued in droves to see them: 'We are pleased to be showing for the first time in over fifty years complete, beautiful 35mm prints of Laurel and Hardy classics!' *The Return of Laurel and Hardy* consists of the original uncut versions of *Duck Soup* (1927), *You're Darn Tootin'* (1928), *Habeas Corpus* (1928), *Big Business* (1929), *Double Whoopee* (1929) and *Liberty* (1929).

The revival of Laurel and Hardy's work in the United States came in the late fifties. Once their films had been shown on television, Stan and Ollie acquired a bigger public than they had ever had before, almost overnight. Their humour was still something people understood and appreciated: in an American 'Dennis the Menace' comic strip of the time, Dennis has the television on and is excitedly phoning up a friend: 'Hey Tommy! Turn on Channel Four! There's two new funny guys called Laurel and Hardy!'

An international Laurel and Hardy fan club was set up in America and called 'Sons of the Desert' after the film they made in 1933. Individual sections of the club are called 'tents' and named after other Laurel and Hardy films. After all this time, the duo still have cult status,

Come Clean (1931). Laurel
and Hardy save Mae Busch
from suicide.

not only in America but throughout the world. Their films are hired and
sold on video and appear frequently on television, articles and books on
their films are still being published, the scripts of their short films are
being published in collected form, and although the many records and
cassettes of their soundtracks may not make the Top Twenty (with one
or two exceptions) they continue to sell well. Anything remotely
connected with them has a market: Laurel and Hardy pencil sharpeners,
mirrors, diaries and pictures.

In 1975 Delos Records (855 Via de la Plaza, Pacific Palisades,
California 90272, USA) published an interview between Tony Thomas
and Stan Laurel given in January 1959 in Santa Monica. It is intriguing to
hear Stan recount how he played walk-on parts in the Metropole
Theatre in Glasgow as his introduction to the world of show business.
His description of the relationship between himself and Oliver Hardy
(whom he calls 'Babe') is also a fascinating insight into the way the
legendary comic duo actually worked. For example they rarely
socialized with each other outside the studio, and if there was a gap
between the making of two films they might not see each other for a
month at a time. Their two personalities were very different as well.
Oliver preferred to have nothing to do with the organization and
editing of their films and never stayed in the studio a moment longer
than he had to, whilst Stan was often a major source of inspiration and
guidance during the production process. Oliver relaxed by playing golf,
working in the garden, betting on horses and watching sport, often
accompanied by Hal Roach. Laurel and Hardy were very fond of each
other, but not friends in the way their screen partnership might suggest.
It is clear that Stan Laurel was the more creative of the two, and he was
paid more than Oliver Hardy. He had his own office in the Hal Roach

studios and would often burn the midnight oil in the cutting room with Richard Currier or Bert Jordan, or sit behind the piano with composer T. Marvin Hatley. It was Hatley that wrote the theme tune that everyone knows, the 'Cuckoo Song' (tum-tum-tee-tum, tum-tum-tee-tum) and the background music to many of their films, the 'Our Gang' series and other Hal Roach comedies. In *Film Collector's World* dated 15 October 1982, we read that the man who wrote the 'Cuckoo Song' was producing another LP, this time called 'Music for Laurel and Hardy (and friends)', with extracts from Laurel and Hardy's soundtracks and six new compositions based on themes from the duo's classic Hal Roach comedies. The LP is personally signed by T. Marvin Hatley: a collector's item, and proof that the house composer of Hal Roach Studios is atill active in his profession after all this time: he was born in 1905 (the record is obtainable from T. Marvin Hatley, 7308 Filmore Drive, Buena Park, California 90620, USA).

You're Darn Tootin (1928).

The chances of any reader not having seen at least one film, or part of a film made by Laurel and Hardy are remote, to say the least: rarely a month goes by without one being shown on television. And although Stan and Oliver are dead now, the contents of their films have been recounted and analysed on countless occasions since; background details of their lives are still being published and directors are still interviewed on the way they worked with Laurel and Hardy. All the regulars from their films are now dead: Mae Busch (1897-1946),

Rychard Cramer (1889-1960), Billy Gilbert (1893-1971), Charlie Hall (1899-1959), Arthur Housman (1888-1942), Edgar Kennedy (1890-1981), Walter Long (1879-1952), Daphne Pollard (1890-1978) and Tiny San(d)ford (1894-1961). So the fountain of knowledge about Laurel and Hardy is fast drying up.

Another way to appreciate the duo is to visit streets and areas of Culver City in Los Angeles where Laurel and Hardy films were once made. The staircase from the three-reeler *The Music Box,* made in 1932 is still there, just as it was more than half a century ago. This historic site is on Vendome Street, between numbers 923 and 925. It is fascinating to think that these are the very same 131 stairs up which Stan and Ollie struggled in 1932 with a pianola packed in a box, even though the box was empty when this hilarious Oscar-winning Hal Roach comedy was filmed.

Another place of pilgrimage for Laurel and Hardy fans is 10281

Dunleer Drive, in Los Angeles. This was the house that Laurel and Hardy almost wrecked when its owner (James Finlayson) refused to order a Christmas tree from them in the middle of summer. When this particular comedy was made (*Big Business,* 1928), the team found an employee of the studio who was willing to take a generous amount of compensation for the damage they did to his home (the window panes and door post had to be replaced and the front of the house repainted). The house has barely changed at all since the time the film was made.

A Haunting We Will Go (1942), the second feature Laurel and Hardy made for 20th Century-Fox.

A sentimental journey through the home of Laurel and Hardy should also include 3120 Vera Avenue, Los Angeles. It was this address that Stan and Oliver leave with their wives (Kay Deslys and Isabelle Keith), their infirm uncle Edgar (Edgar Kennedy) and a rickety old Model T Ford for a day's picnic. Their departure takes an inordinately long time and at one point it seems as though they are never actually going to stop waving and saying goodbye to their neighbours (*Perfect Day,* 1929). Another attraction is the City Hall in Culver City, at 9770 Culver Boulevard, which had a sign reading 'County Hospital' affixed to it for the film of the same name in 1932. First of all, Stan hurtles past the door in his car and almost takes off as he comes to visit Oliver, who is a patient; and at the end of the film the two emerge from the hospital, with Oliver's right leg covered in plaster. The City Hall was also used as a location for *Going Bye Bye* in 1934, where it served as a courthouse. The boating lake in *Men of War* (1929), where Laurel and Hardy conduct a mini sea-battle under the watchful eye of James Finlayson, can also be seen between St Louis Street and 4th Street in Hollenbeck Park.

If you are one of those people who has seen every Laurel and

Swiss Miss (1938).

Blockheads (1938).

Hardy film ten times and knows all the books on the subject off by heart, you may be interested in *A Guide to Laurel and Hardy Movie Locations,* an excellent A4-sized book with plenty of photos and maps. It is published by Leon Smith, of 6519 Paseo El Greco, Anaheim Hills, California 92807, USA.

In comparison with, say, Charlie Chaplin or W. C. Fields, little is known about the private lives of Stan Laurel and Oliver Hardy. Although by the time they reached the pinnacle of their careers between 1930 and 1940 they were very well known and very popular, the public did not put them in the same bracket as the type of Hollywood star who captured the imagination and got columns written about him or her in the film magazines. Stan Laurel left one daughter, Lois, who still occasionally appears at Laurel and Hardy conferences in America. She was born in 1928, and two years later Stan Junior (Stanley Robert Jefferson) was born, though he lived for only nine days. Stan successively married Lois Neilson (1926), Virginia Ruth Rogers (1934 and again in 1941), Vera Ivanova Shuvalova (1938) and finally Ida Kitaeva Raphael (1946), who stayed with him until his death in 1965. Oliver married three times: first Madelyn Saloshin (they were together from 1913 to 1917), then Myrtle Lee Reeves (1921-37), and finally Lucille Jones (from 1940 until Oliver's death in 1957). In addition, Oliver appears to have had a serious affair with a young mother who, like him, came from the Deep South: Viola Morse.

Because in principle Stan Laurel and Oliver Hardy were contracted to Hal Roach Studios, and later on to 20th Century-Fox, they never had distribution rights to their films in the way that Chaplin and Harold Lloyd did. Stan Laurel in particular was always angry about this unprofitable situation: for example, their films could be shown on television without either of them receiving a cent. The story surrounding their film rights is lengthy and full of anomalies, and currently different terms apply depending on where the films are to be shown: in private households where they are not shown for profit, rental to schools and clubs not generally open to the public, cinema showings, television, and video. The rights for each of these categories have passed through very many hands since the films were first made.

In America, the films make such frequent appearances on almost every TV channel that some of them have been given a new dimension by the addition of computerized colouring. Two companies, Color Systems Technology in Los Angeles and rivals Colorization in Toronto have now added colour to a number of Laurel and Hardy shorts, including *County Hospital* (1932) and *The Fixer Uppers* (1935). The results, surprisingly enough, are strikingly good. They still have a period feel to them, like Victorian hand-coloured prints, that gives them added visual interest and yet preserves their nostalgia value. If we may be allowed a little pedantry, the real Stan Laurel had red hair and very light blue eyes. In the coloured versions of his films, he is given brown hair and brown eyes: probably someone pressing the wrong button in the video laboratory.

When Abbott and Costello appeared on the scene, Laurel and Hardy suddenly found they had competition. Their monopoly in the field of two-man comedy was threatened in 1940, when Universal International brought out *One Night in the Tropics* and a year later *Buck Privates*, in which Bud Abbott and Lou Costello first made their names together as film comedians. Laurel and Hardy made a similar comedy based on the army, *Great Guns*, for 20th Century-Fox in 1941. Under the direction of Monty Banks, it turned out as a middle-of-the-road film which did not draw audiences. Now, more than forty years on, it comes across as an excellent B-movie, but at the time the more 'modern' comedy team of Abbott and Costello had a greater appeal than the 'old-fashioned' Laurel and Hardy. It is perhaps unfair to ascribe Stan and Oliver's lack of success after 1941 solely to the fact that they had moved to 20th Century-Fox, where they made *Great Guns, A Haunting We Will Go, Jitterbugs, The Dancing Masters, The Big Noise,* and *The Bullfighters.* When they left Hal Roach, mainly for financial reasons and because he was astute enough to realize that their popularity might be on the wane, Stan Laurel was fifty, and Oliver Hardy forty-eight. Not a great age for a lawyer or an artist, perhaps, but it was as far as a film

comedian was concerned. Stan had probably had enough of playing the naive, somewhat limp persona that he did, whilst Oliver Hardy's fat, bossy character was starting to look ridiculous rather than merely hilarious. The more successful Abbott and Costello became, the more Laurel and Hardy's popularity faded. When they began their last and worst film, *Atoll K,* in 1950, Stan Laurel was sixty and Oliver Hardy fifty-eight. Apart from Abbott and Costello they now also had to contend with the comic duo from Paramount Pictures, Dean Martin and Jerry Lewis. The cinema-going public was starting to give Stan and Oliver the cold shoulder, and their career was at an end. Less than ten years later, the tide turned: in the late fifties and early sixties, their comedies started to be shown on television and they underwent a gigantic revival, with public appreciation of their pre-1940 films being renewed. Whilst their rivals at the time were by then largely unremembered and only now are starting to be rediscovered, for Stan Laurel and Oliver Hardy this was a peak in their careers just as great as that which they had experienced three decades before.

6

W.C. Fields:
The eccentric juggler

W.C. Fields was never quite as popular on this side of the Atlantic as comedians like Laurel and Hardy and Abbott and Costello. The fact is that, despite the power of his comic genius, he told the public he detested dogs and children, and this is not the kind of remark which is calculated to endear yourself to an audience.

Fields never fitted in with his surroundings, either as a child or an

W.C. Fields.

adult. He distrusted everything and everyone, hated his birthplace
Philadelphia so much that he did not even want to be buried there, and
spent his time continually insulting and offending those around him.
The only thing he did feel an affinity for was the bottle. This, at least,
was how he is portrayed in the biographies of Hollywood's greatest
grumbler.

Nor are the conventional descriptions of his life wholly without
foundation. Bill Field's colleagues produced a number of books about
the most aggressive and cynical comedian Hollywood has ever known.
Then, in 1976, Universal made *W. C. Fields and Me,* a film based on the
memoirs of Mexican actress, Carlotta Monti, who was Fields' lover for
the last fourteen years of his life. In the film, the role of Woody Fields
(Carlotta's nickname for him) is superbly portrayed by Rod Steiger.
Not only does Steiger bear a very close physical resemblance to Fields:
he also manages to imitate to perfection the slightly strange, slow,
musical voice: 'By all meaeaensss, yeas, indeeeed...!' The result is a
script which often consists of unintelligible mumbling.

W. C. Fields and Me shows vaudeville actor Bill Fields as a drink-

One of the best stills of the 'real' W.C. Fields, taken in 1937.

sodden, scheming, vain and shady showman. At the same time, he is an actor of genius, a sensitive and vulnerable artist, someone who can bring out people's sympathy for the underdog (his friendship with the German dwarf, Ludwig, is movingly portrayed in the film), and is able to maintain good relations with fellow professionals in the field such as actor John Barrymore, director Leo McCarey and director/producer Eddie Sutherland.

The film tells the story of W.C. Fields through the eyes of Carlotta Monti. Film historians have pointed out that Monti knew him for 'only' fourteen years, and for a long time she was unaware of the existence of Harriet Hughes, whom he married on 8 April 1900, and of the birth of his son, William Claude Fields Junior, on 28 July 1904. Later, in 1927, Fields had another son by *Ziegfeld Follies* beauty, Bessie Pool. When Carlotta found out, Woody said to his 'Chinaman' (his nickname for her, based on the fact that she was particularly good at playing Eastern roles in her revues), 'A night of pleasure can cause a swollen abdomen nine months later!'

In vain did members of Fields' family protest to Universal about the contents and scope of the film. The job of burying him when he died fell to his legal wife, Harriet, and her son William. It happened on the day he detested most of all: Christmas, and in direct contravention of his wishes, which he often impressed on Carlotta Monti: 'I don't want any funeral. Just cremate me. I had enough of the cold ground in my youth!'

William Claude Dukenfield (some sources maintain his name was originally Dukinfield) was born some time around 1879 in Philadelphia. There are three different versions of his exact birthdate: 10 February 1879, 28 June 1879 and 29 January 1880. He was born to a poor immigrant family where the arrival of the first child (another half-dozen followed) was an event of little or no importance. On 5 June 1880, a council official recorded laconically in the city's register: 'A child approximately five months old named William Claude Dukenfield was in residence with his parents at 6320 Woodland Avenue, Philadelphia.'

As a boy, he received hardly any education, but even before his ninth birthday he had become a skilled conjurer and juggler and by the time he was fourteen he had run away from home and was putting his ability to use in fairs and travelling variety shows. He also had a passion for billiards and golf. During his teenage years he started his acting career playing in second-rate melodramas, and this experience stood him in good stead when he first appeared on film. He also worked as a hustler

The Old-Fashioned Way (1934): W.C. Fields, playing The Great McGonigle.

in a pool room, playing for money: his function was to play very badly
until some unfortunate tried to take advantage of his inability at the
game, whereupon the hustler would beat the newcomer hands down
and scoop up all the winnings. It was a tough life which involved a good
deal of sleeping rough and stealing money and food: for a time he was
even in prison. The bulbous nose which was to become his trademark
was the result not of excessive drinking, but of street fighting. He was
an outsider, not greatly liked by his fellow-citizens, and Fields likewise
made no secret of his antipathy to Philadelphia. In interviews, and the
radio shows he did for NBC with Edgar Bergen and his dummy,
'Charlie McCarthy', from 1937 to 1944, he never missed an
opportunity to mention his birthplace: 'Last weekend I went to
Philadelphia, but it was closed!'

By 1905, W.C. Fields was a well-known vaudeville figure both in
America and Europe. His letterheadings of the time were indicative of
the variety of roles he played: 'William Claude Fields, Silent Humorist';
'William C. Fields, Tramp Juggler'; 'W. Claude Fields, the
Distinguished Comedian'; W.C. Fields, the Eccentric Juggler'. Between
1909 and 1914 he drew cartoons for advertisements and articles that
appeared about him in local newspapers; they are skilfully drawn and
this was another facet of Fields' talent.

In 1915, Fields made his first short film, *Pool Sharks,* for the English
company Gaumont in New York. This consisted mainly of scenes from
his billiard act, the trick shots which had helped him to establish his
reputation on the stage and in the pool rooms. But it was not until ten
years later that his real film career got under way, in a film directed by
D.W. Griffith, *Sally of the Sawdust,* where Fields plays Professor
Eustace McGargie in a film version of the Broadway musical *Poppy,*
which he had played to packed houses night after night in 1923. Earlier,
between 1915 and 1921, he had joined the *Ziegfeld Follies* and *George's
White Scandals.*

By the time he left music hall and variety in favour of the new
medium of cinema, Fields was a very respected and well-known stage
artist, and like Laurel and Hardy the transition from silent films to
talkies was an effortless one. His first talkie, *The Golf Specialist,* was a
twenty-minute two-reeler made for RKO in 1930. This, and the shorts
he wrote and starred in for Mack Sennett during 1932 and 1933 (*The
Dentist, The Fatal Glass of Beer, The Pharmacist* and *The Barber Shop*)
were amongst the best films he ever made. In fact, it is these minor films
of W.C. Fields which are most respected and enjoyed by today's
generation of television viewers.

The Dentist is the prototype W.C. Fields film, a two-reeler in which,
as always, he makes considerable use of material he wrote and used in
his theatre days. First he paces round his house in agony, clutching a
block of ice to his face (and harking back to the days when Fields
worked delivering ice as a child), then goes on to demonstrate one of his
famous golf scenes. When he finally arrives in the dentist's surgery, the
result is one of the all-time classic comedy scenes. The dentist, played by

The Dentist (1932): 'Now, that didn't hurt, did it?'

Fields, wrestles with his patient in an inhuman, almost perversely sadistic manner; the illustrations here show how. Fields had already played this scene in 1918, to a highly receptive *Ziegfeld Follies* audience. The act was so polished, the physical violence so beautifully choreographed, that it was well-nigh inimitable.

Another minor masterpiece, directed by Clyde Bruckman and written and acted by W.C. Fields, was *The Fatal Glass of Beer*. Fields plays the trapper living in a depressing little hut somewhere in the frozen north, wearing gloves as he plays a zither and sings a mournful ballad about his son, Chester, who after drinking a single glass of beer started sliding down the slippery slope to ruin and eventually ended up in prison.

Later, the reprobate Chester comes home and is smothered with affection by his parents.

Chester:	I feel so tired, I think I'll go to bed.
Pa:	Why don't you lie down and take a little rest first, Chester?
Chester:	Well, good night, Pa.
Pa:	Good night, Chester.
Chester:	Good night, Pa.
Ma:	Good night, Chester.
Pa:	Sleep well, Chester.
Chester:	Thank you, Pa, and you too.
Pa:	Thank you, Chester.
Ma:	Sleep well, Chester.
Chester:	Thank you, Ma, and you sleep well.
Pa:	Don't forget to open your window a bit, Chester.
Chester:	Don't forget to open yours a bit, Pa.
Pa:	I won't, Chester.
Ma:	Yes, don't forget to open your window a bit, Chester.
Chester:	Open yours a bit, too, Ma.
Pa and Ma:	Good night, Chester.
Chester:	Good night, Pa, good night, Ma.
Pa:	Good night.
Ma:	Good night.
Pa:	Good night ... Chester.

When his parents discover that their beloved son no longer has the proceeds of his thievery, he is summarily ejected from the cabin. A snow storm is raging outside, and the running joke is that whenever Fields opens the door, an invisible hand throws a handful of fake snow into his face. Fields: 'And it ain't a fit night out for man or beast!'

To the true devotee of W.C. Fields, the four Mack Sennett comedies are extremely funny. At the time, though, when Paramount brought them out in America in the 1930s as shorts to accompany a main feature, they were not popular; many cinema-owners complained to the distributors that they found the plot and the humour weak. Wrote one theatre-owner in Michigan: 'Two reels of film and twenty minutes wasted!'

It was not until the 1970s that a W.C. Fields cult gradually grew up in the colleges of New York City, where people started to realize how funny Fields still was, and continued in the city's smaller independent cinemas. W.C. Fields is now something of an idol amongst young intellectuals whose respect he shares with Lenny Bruce and Woody Allen. An ability to quote from his utterances is a *sine qua non*, and classics like 'I never drink water, fish fuck in it!' and 'I exercise complete self-control, I never drink anything stronger than gin before breakfast' are part of almost any anthology of famous sayings. The authenticity of some of his quotes has been cast into doubt, though: some say that it was not Fields, but Leo Rosten, who said, 'Any man who hates small dogs and children can't be all bad!'

Although the process of growing old severely affected the ability of many comedians to make their audiences laugh – Stan Laurel, Buster Keaton and Harry Langdon all relied on their fresh-faced innocence for humorous effect – advancing age had no effect whatsoever upon Fields' charismatic presence. When he was sixty he made *The Bank Dick*, one of his funniest films, which he wrote under the pseudonym of Mahatma Kane Jeeves, one of his many bizarre *noms de plume*. He was fifty-eight when he appeared in *Poppy*, a brilliant film in which he sells a filthy mongrel to a publican. When Fields places his order, the dog also asks for a drink: his 'owner' is, of course, a ventriloquist. The publican is fascinated by the idea of a talking dog and excited by its commercial possibilities, so he buys it. No sooner has the money changed hands, than the dog, piqued by its master's betrayal, is made to say, 'Just for that, I'll never talk again!' Says Fields anxiously to the new owner, 'Stubborn little fellow, he probably means it, too!' and walks out of the bar with the money in his hand.

The fact that W.C. Fields was obviously able to continue in his profession until such a late age, drawing endless inspiration from his spite and inbuilt misanthropy, probably comes from his thorough training at an early age in the art of vaudeville. Performing magic with cards, balls, coins, bottles, hats and other props was an almost daily activity, and during pauses in filming he would often perform tricks to amuse friend and foe alike. His fingers were fat, but could move like lightning, and this also stood him in good stead when he cheated at cards, something he learned at an early age and practised all his life. His quick-fire verbal wit and repartee was also something he learned in his youth when he often had to appear in front of rowdy, half-drunk audiences in the music hall.

Stories of Fields' dependence on alcohol are legion. Louise Brooks, a colleague who worked with him on a number of films including *It's the Old Army Game* (1926) recounts in her book, *Lulu in Hollywood*, that it did not become a problem until the latter years of his life. Most of his career passed without any need for the demon drink, and Fields detested being on the set with anyone else who was drunk. This may well be the case, for magicians and the like who use their hands to make a living must obviously avoid having shaking hands because of over-indulgence, and in variety, drink is generally taboo. Fields had worked too hard to earn a professional reputation to be able to afford to lose it through drink.

Nevertheless, Fields liked to keep up the image of a drunkard. It gave him *carte blanche* to insult his audiences: 'Fields is drunk, don't listen to him, he doesn't know what he's talking about!' Nor is it true that it was

Never Give a Sucker an Even Break (1941): Irving Bacon is worried about his customer's state of health.

drink which made his voice so hoarse and difficult to understand: when he was a child, he was often forced to sleep in ditches or damp sheds, and frequently suffered from throat infections. Even before his twentieth birthday, his vocal chords were damaged and, ironically, this was also the reason for his great skill at ventriloquism. It gave him just as much pleasure to preserve the myth that he hated children. When he died, 'Uncle' Fields left $800,000, distributed across more than seven hundred bank accounts throughout the world, to build an orphanage for children of all religions. Fields had a dread of finding himself in a town at home or abroad without any money, so placed his money in different banks wherever he went. He even had around $50,000 in banks in Nazi Germany, and is supposed to have replied to anyone who asked him why, 'Just in case that bastard wins!'

A cartoon drawn by Fields in 1913 to illustrate an article on 'The Eccentric Juggler', i.e. himself

W.C. Fields very distinctive style has variously been described as cynical, sour, surly, embittered, snarling, and any number of adjectives one would not normally associate with a humorist. Both on screen and off it, Fields constantly expressed his dislike of the human race and his hatred for the establishment, for bureaucracy and convention. Physically, too, his paunch arrogantly thrust out, his small, grim, watchful eyes, small, pursed lips and large pug nose, were the picture of misery and sadness (at least when he grew older, for the young W.C. Fields was surprisingly good-looking). He kept up a constant barrage of invective against an idealized version of family life and the false respectability of middle class existence. W.C. Fields was actually playing himself: no one knows where the real Fields stops and the actor Fields takes over. In Fields, we see a brilliant comic talent residing in the body of a little-liked rancorous man, but even half a century later the public can still identify with him.

A final insight into the character of W.C. Fields. In 1933, he appeared in *Tillie and Gus* with Baby LeRoy, an unlikeable small child who he is constantly at loggerheads with. The story has it that the child scratched Fields in the face during a rehearsal (Fields: 'That bastard's going to be the first four-year-old in Alcatraz!'). In revenge, Uncle Bill Fields spiked the child's drink of orange juice with whisky, with the result that Baby LeRoy ended up staggering drunkenly around the stage, to the great delight of Fields.

I hope none of you are laughing at that story . . .

7

Lucille Ball: Sitmom

In books on the history of the cinema, Mack Sennett is often called The King of Comedy, a title which was justly earned and which he was proud to bear. If Sennett is the King, the Queen of Comedy must surely be Lucille Ball.

On 15 October 1951, Columbia Broadcasting System (CBS) broadcast the first episode of a new series: 'I Love Lucy', called 'The

Girls Want to Go to a Nightclub'. Twenty-three years later, on the cover of the world's biggest-selling listings magazine, *TV Guide* dated 6 July 1974, there is a portrait of Lucille Ball, captioned: 'End of an Era: Lucy Bows Out After 23 years!'

During those twenty-three years, Lucille Ball made so many television programmes that it would take around ten whole days to show them continuously. There have been three different versions of her situation-comedy series: 179 episodes of 'I Love Lucy', 156 of 'The Lucy Show', and 144 of 'Here is Lucy'. Lucy was forty when she began her television career, but she already had twenty years of show business behind her. She began playing decorative bit parts in feature films for RKO, MGM and Columbia, and ended up so rich that she and her husband Desi Arnaz where able to buy the former RKO studios at 780 North Gower Street in Hollywood and set up their own film and television company, Desilu, the name being a combination of their own names. Within a year it was a multi-million-dollar company. Lucy and Desi, their three resident scriptwriters Jess Oppenheimer, Madalyn Pugh and Bob Carroll, long-time supporting actors Vivian Vance and William Frawley, and chief cameraman Karl Freund, who had worked for German directors such as Fritz Lang, F. W. Murnau and Erich Pommer, went on to work on 'The Lucy Show' with renewed enthusiasm in the studio they had bought.

Kid Millions (1934): Lucille Ball (second from right) as a member of Busby Berkeley's Goldwyn Girls.

The series was bought for $30,000 in 1951 by cigarette mogul Philip Morris, and without giving it a great deal of thought, CBS agreed to Desi Arnaz and Lucille Ball's request that they be given the broadcasting rights. This was the worst decision CBS ever made, but at the time neither they nor the two other networks, ABC and NBC, saw much potential in a TV series where an average American housewife marries a man with a Spanish accent who has achieved a modest amount of recognition as a Latin American bandleader. CBS wanted the series to be called 'The Lucille Ball Show', but Lucille wanted her husband's name to appear before her own. Finally they arrived at a compromise, and it became 'I Love Lucy': the 'I' referred to Desi Arnaz, so Lucille Ball was happy.

Philip Morris, the sponsors, wanted to screen the shows live and were particularly anxious that viewers in New York City should have perfect reception, since it was there that the highest number of cigarette-smokers and potential nicotine addicts lived. But this would have meant the crew and cast moving to CBS studios in New York, and

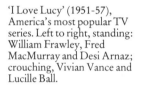

'I Love Lucy' (1951-57), America's most popular TV series. Left to right, standing: William Frawley, Fred MacMurray and Desi Arnaz; crouching, Vivian Vance and Lucille Ball.

Desi and Lucy emphatically protested against the idea. There were no video recorders, and the Kinescope system in use at the time, based on a cathode-ray tube, tended to give a somewhat grey, watery and blurred picture. Veteran cameraman Karl Freund suggested that the programmes be recorded in front of a studio audience using four 35mm film cameras with 900-metre film cassettes, all filming simultaneously so that each could show one particular section of the action.

Most of the action in the programme takes place in the living-room and neighbouring kitchen, situated at 623 East 68th Street in New York. It is filmed so that the viewer is in effect watching through a transparent fourth wall, and the result is very much like watching a stage play. But the photography, lighting, editing and timing are all cinematic, just as Karl Freund advised. The superbly made 35mm films of the series were packed into drums and sent off to television stations not only in America, but all over the world.

The humour of Lucille Ball, 'the clown with glamour', caught on instantly with TV viewers, with the reassuring workaday cares of

Postcard of the RKO Studios in Hollywood which Lucille Ball and Desi Arnaz bought in 1958 for their company, Desilu.

Desi and Lucy Ricardo, their son Ricky and neighbours, the Mertez family. Lucy wants to get into films, and Desi is the $150-a-week bandleader at the Tropicana nightclub. Ricky, who is often called Mickey by Lucy's mother, Mrs MacGillicuddy, is a smaller-scale version of Desi who spends all day indefatigably bashing away at his drum kit. The role is played by six-year-old Keith Thibodeaux, 'the world's tiniest professional drummer'. Desi's Spanish accent is not an act but the way he speaks in reality, though he could easily do something about it if he tried. But it is used to considerable comic effect. On Arnaz' dressing-room door in the Desilu studios there was a sign which read: 'English broken here!'.

It is not unusual nowadays to be switching back and forth between channels on a TV set in America and see five programmes with Lucille Ball in one day. The classic sitcoms such as 'Lucy's Italian Movie', 'Job Switchin'' and 'Lucy Goes to the Hospital' are amongst those most often repeated. Lucy's devotees claim that every single episode is a hit, and certainly none of them can be called really unexciting. They cite scenes such as Lucy dressing up as Superman on Ricky's birthday, and out of the blue bumping into the real Superman, every young American TV viewer's idol at the time. Another episode which her fans classify as one of the all-time greats is when Lucy and Ethel start work in a sweet factory (Kramer's Candy Kitchen) packing sweets on a conveyor belt. But the conveyor belt is too fast for them and in a panic they start stuffing sweets into their blouses and mouths. This is pure slapstick, acted by two skilled all-round comediennes who, at the time, were being watched by audiences larger than comedians such as Charley Chase and Harry Langdon every enjoyed in the space of several years with their short films.

'The Lucy Show' (1961-68): Lucy with Mr Television USA', Milton Berle.

Before she made such a big hit on television, Lucille Ball played with such famous artists as The Three Stooges, in their two-reeler *Three Little Pigskins* (1934), and Leon Errol in his comedy, *Perfectly Mismated* (1934). She acted with Fred Astaire and Ginger Rogers in *Roberta* (1935), *Top Hat* (1935) and *Follow the Fleet* (1936). Although she has more that fifty films to her credit, Lucille never reached superstar status; it was not until she started appearing on television that she reached the big time, at a fairly late age for an actress. On 28 November 1976, CBS broadcast a special programme, 'CBS Salutes Lucy', produced by her second husband, Gary Morton. In the programme, she says: 'Stardom came late, my children Desi and Ricky came late. It's like the first twenty years in Hollywood didn't exist!'

The Godmother of TV comedy or, as some christened her, 'Sitmom', was spoken to on a large-scale TV screen by colleagues such as Danny Kaye, Dick Van Dyke, Dean Martin, Bob Hope, John Wayne, Carol Burnett and her ex-husband (from whom she was divorced in February 1960) Desi Arnaz. Lucy was so moved, she cried.

Her near-neighbour James Stewart – he lives at 918 Roxbury Drive in Hollywood, and she at No. 1000 – gave her a plaque on behalf of the Academy of Television Arts and Sciences, reading: 'Thank you for the greatest gift anyone can give us: laughter!' And she was happy, even if she had an entire cupboard full of awards at home already, including her Emmys, the TV version of an Oscar.

Once Desi Arnaz and Lucille Ball split up, they both took a short rest from television. She appeared in a New York musical, *Wildcat*, and it was here that she met her second husband, Gary Morton. On 8 November 1962, she took over Desi Arnaz' shares in Desilu and became the sole owner of the company, by now a well-oiled machine producing episodes of America's (and therefore the world's) best-known TV series. At Gary Morton's insistence, she began a new series, 'The Lucy Show', this time with Vivian Vance as her partner instead of Desi Arnaz. The addition of Gale Gordon as Mr Mooney was also a felicitous choice.

In 'The Lucy Show', Lucille Ball plays Lucy Carmichael and Vivian Vance is Vivian Bagley. They are both widowed; Lucy has two children (Chris and Jerry) and Vivian one (Sherman). Eventually the show was rebaptized 'Here's Lucy', and her real children, Desi Junior and Lucy, played their fictional equivalents. The combination of Lucille Ball and Vivian Vance was a good one; she was a year older than Lucy and functioned as a self-effacing 'straight man' for Lucille, the comedienne. Lucy and Viv were the new Zasu Pitts and Patsy Kelly, originally launched by Hal Roach as 'the female Laurel and Hardy'. Stan Laurel was a great fan of Lucy's during his latter years and loved to watch her on television with his wife, Ida.

Lucille Ball was born in 1911 and has therefore reached a considerable age by now. Although she is not currently active in television, she is a 'living legend', invited to appear on chat shows and constantly interviewed by newspapers and magazines. She still takes pleasure in watching reruns of her various series, and she and Desi Arnaz still receive royalties whenever they are shown.

In the early 1970s Lucille Ball sold Desilu Studios to Gulf and Western Industries, which since 1966 has owned companies including Paramount. She is only moderately enthusiastic about the new brand of comedy she sees on the TV screen, and it is difficult to deny that she herself was a better actress than people who are given star billing nowadays. In her own series she was able to do a magnificent impression of Harpo Marx (with her own superb mirror scene), as well as Charlie Chaplin, Tallulah Bankhead and a third of the Andrews Sisters.

More than three thousand actors and actresses appeared in Lucille Ball's shows at one time or another. It was always a great honour to be invited to appear, and many of the true greats of the cinema screen made appearances, sometimes in very minor roles. Amongst the guest stars welcomed onto her show were Buster Keaton, Charles Boyer, Orson Wells, Betty Grable, Maurice Chevalier, Rudy Vallee, Tennessee Ernie Ford, Bob Cummings, Fred MacMurray and many others.

From her fifteenth birthday onwards, Lucille Ball's life was one incessant round of work, often day and night. The marriage to Desi Arnaz did not work well: he was unable to resist other females' charms or the smell of whisky, and was thus rarely at home.

One person who realized at a very early stage that Lucille was going to make it to the top in show business was the comedian Eddie Cantor. In *Roman Scandals* (1933) Lucy is a member of a dance troupe, and the script called for a lump of mud to be thrown at Cantor. He bends down and the mud flies straight into the surprised face of one of the dancing girls. Who would volunteer for this thankless task? None of the leggy dancers was particularly enthusiastic about the idea, but Lucille Ball stepped resolutely forward. Whereupon Cantor said: 'Get that girl's name. That's the one who will make it!'

He was right too. In fact, she became so famous that in 1953 the front pages of newspapers carried the headline: 'Lucille Ball Named Red!' Television news programmes carried still photographs of her: 'America's top comedienne has been confronted with membership of the Communist party!'

In her defence, Lucy stated that she had joined in 1936 'to please my grandfather'. Nevertheless she was accused of 'Un-American activities', as were others of her colleagues. Much has been written about the Communist witch-hunt: anyone appearing on the blacklist had to find themselves another job. Lucille took the accusations badly and it was a miserable phase in her life: she neither wanted to work, nor was she able to.

She was given considerable support by the sponsor of 'I Love Lucy', the Philip Morris Company, which unexpectedly stood behind her in her fight to clear her name. CBS refused to screen her show until the commission had reached a verdict. A few minutes before the programme was due to go out live (the shows were not pre-recorded),

'The Lucy Show' (1961-68): Lucy imitates TV comedian Ernie Kovacs (left). Right: Desi Arnaz.

Lucy was cleared. During the warm-up to the show, Desi Arnaz made an emotional speech to the studio audience: 'Lucille Ball is no Communist! Lucy has never been a Communist, not now and never will be. Please, ladies and gentlemen, don't believe every piece of junk you read in today's newspapers!'

The audience gave him a standing ovation and there was much blowing of noses. Then Arnaz announced: 'And now I want you to meet my favourite wife – my favourite redhead in fact, and that's the only thing red about her, and even that's not legitimate!'

The instigators of the McCarthy witch-hunt were forced to climb down somewhat. Desi Arnaz had stated earlier that he would buy programme time from the three main TV networks on a weekly basis to fight the accusers of America's most loved comedienne from coast to coast, to the bitter end if need be. Mr and Mrs Arnaz had both the financial means and the necessary know-how to wage this unusual war, and they were supported in it by the world's best copywriters and the doyen of cameraman, Karl Freund, who had learned the power of the visual image all those years ago in Germany. Although ultimately it was not necessary, the two most popular television comics of the time, Lucille Ball and Desi Arnaz, would have been perfectly capable of carrying out their threat.

It is worth remembering, too, that they eventually managed to get the 'laughing machine', that apparatus for creating instant hilarity, into the TV industry's studios.

8

The Three Stooges:
Knockabout humour

It has often been said in the medical profession that humour is an ideal therapy for the disturbed personality. Anyone watching a film by The Three Stooges for the first time would come away thinking that here were three people, themselves severely disturbed, trying to make other people laugh. Nor would The Three Stooges themselves have put up with any intellectual definition of what humour is all about: their formula, which they applied with total success to their films, was to make the largest possible number of people laugh as often as possible.

Between 1930 and 1958, The Three Stooges were the most distinctive and most successful trio of film comedians in the industry, as well as the most prolific. They made 24 full-length features, 191 shorts and many guest appearances in other people's films. When television arrived, ABC began broadcasting 30 two-reelers by the Stooges, beginning in October 1949, after they had bought the broadcasting rights fairly cheaply from Columbia. Ten years later, 85 local TV stations showed all their shorts in quick succession, and even now in 1987 their films can still be seen almost daily on American TV. In fact, they have never been as popular as they are today – this is as true of The Three Stooges as it is of many of the other comedians mentioned in this book. The medium of television needs so much material to keep the public's screens filled that there is a thriving market in old B-movies. These have the dual advantage of being unfamiliar, and therefore of entertainment value, to the younger generation, and familiar to their elders who can take a nostalgic pleasure in them. So the films are almost guaranteed to be a success with their audience, and they are cheap as far as the television industry is concerned.

How High is Up? (1940). Left to right: Larry Fine, Moe Howard and Curly Howard.

The Three Stooges Meet Hercules (1961). Left to right: Joe de Rita, Moe Howard and Larry Fine.

The Three Stooges' films are physical comedy, so much so that in America they were dubbed 'the wildest trio in the history of American entertainment'. Their humour is pitiless; they create chaos wherever they go and insult anyone who falls foul of them in totally unambiguous fashion (one Stooge, to a waiter when paying the bill in a restaurant: 'Sonny, remind me to murder you later!'). They have as little pity for each other as for their enemies, their favourite terms of endearment are words like 'weasel', 'featherbrain', 'dumb-bell', 'porcupine', 'mongoose'. They constantly attack each other physically as well; their scripts are full of directions like 'double cheek slap', 'poke in the eyes', 'triple slap', 'nose tweak' and 'forehead slap'.

After initially having worked for Metro-Goldwyn-Mayer, the team moved in 1934 to Columbia Pictures, run by Harry Cohn who was one of their greatest fans. Columbia employees had a nickname for Cohn: His Crudeness. The Stooges made around 190 shorts with Cohn's expert staff, as well as 10 features; their remaining features were made with other film companies. More than half a century after their début in the American studio, they are still frequently shown in the cinema and on the TV screen. Many a modern feature film by Columbia is preceded by a two-reeler from the Stooges in the drive-ins of America. When the opening titles, with their Commedia dell'Arte masks in the background, appear on the wide screen the sides of the image are blank: the films were made in the classic 3:4 ratio, but they are still greeted as enthusiastically as ever: the laugh's the main thing. When they are shown on television, they seem to have a particular appeal for children. The sadistic humour of The Three Stooges is real to them, just

Micro Phonics (1945), with Larry Fine at the piano, Moe Howard playing the flute and Curly singing.

like Tom and Jerry cartoons: anything can happen, anything is possible. If one of the team hits another with a sledgehammer (with a loud bang from the sound-effects man), the victim says archly in close-up: 'Ouch', then kicks his assailant or pokes him accurately in one or both eyes. Then the two will go off the best of friends to meet with new, even more violent adventures.

> Moe: Tell me, do you like the radio?
> Curly: Certainly! I love it!
> Moe: You got it!

Whereupon Curly is hit loudly over the head with a bulky wooden radio set (*Idle Roomers,* 1944).

> Moe: What are you doin'?
> Curly: Listenin' to the band.
> Moe: Would you like to hear some birdies?
> Curly: I'd love it!
> Moe: Take off your hat...

Moe hits Curly on the temples with both fists and there is an audible thud. Curly goes cross-eyed with the shock and we hear joyful birdsong (*Crash Goes the Hash,* 1944).

Watching any Stooges film can be a confusing experience, and it is often hard to make sense of the plot having seen one. Writing about The Three Stooges is further complicated by the fact that the members of the

trio were not always the same: in total, there were actually six. Stooge
No. 1 was Moe Howard (1897-1975), who started with the team in
1925 and continued right up to 1969. No. 2 was Larry Fine (1902-75),
who also started in 1925 and was still being a Stooge on stage and TV in
1969. Stooge No. 3 was Curly Howard (1903-52), who started in 1932
and left in 1946. As far as Stooges buffs are concerned, these three –
Moe, Larry and Curly – were the true Stooges, and it was they who
made the best of the Stooges comedies between 1932 and 1946. Their
two-reeler, *Men in Black,* a parody of the feature film, *Men in White,*
was actually nominated for an Oscar in 1934. In 1946 Stooge No. 4,
Shemp Howard (1895-1955) replaced No. 3, Curly Howard, Stooge
No. 5, Joe Besser (1907-72) replaced No. 4, Shemp Howard, in 1956,
No. 6, Joe DeRita (b.1909) took over from No. 5 Joe Besser, in 1958.
After The Three Stooges finally stopped making films, various
combinations of American comedians tried to continue the success of
the trio. For a short period in 1974, The New Three Stooges made
nightclub appearances: this time they consisted of No. 6 from the
original trio, Joe DeRita, plus Frank Mitchell and Mousie Garner. But
Joe DeRita, then sixty-five years old, had to leave for health reasons and
the trio finally folded.

Back in 1923 there were only two Stooges. Moe and Shemp Howard
were doing a 'black face' act in the show of vaudeville headliner, Ted
Healy. The Howard brothers were billed as Ted Healy and his Stooges.
In 1928 Larry Fine joined the group and then there were three. The
team, which from the outset adopted an aggressive, unrefined, laugh-
or-I'll kill-you brand of humour, appeared with Healy in the film *Soup
to Nuts* (Fox, 1930). Shortly afterwards, Shemp left the Stooges to work
on his own and his place was taken by Jerome (Curly) Howard. After
making seven feature films, The Three Stooges went with producer/
director Jules White to Columbia, and it was here that they made all
their remaining films. Jules White was a very experienced, energetic
film-maker who had a very cordial relationship with the Stooges. When
Harry Cohn offered him a job as head of Columbia's Short Subjects
Department, The Three Stooges went to keep him company. Jules
White was a past master in the art of film-making, having worked as a
gag-writer for Mack Sennett, and one of the first things he did when he
began work with Columbia was to persuade James Horne, another
veteran who directed for the King of Sound Comedy, Hal Roach, to
join the company. As soon as White heard that this former top-notch
comedy director was now working selling cars, he insisted he join
Columbia.

Most of the major Hollywood studios were shutting down their
Short Films departments during the 1950s, but Columbia carried on
regardless. The friendly relations between Jules White and Harry Cohn
was the main reason: according to people who knew them both, White
was the only person Cohn really liked. What was more, Columbia's
two-reelers (which apart from The Three Stooges also featured
comedians such as Leon Errol and Andy Clyde) were consistently

successful and made a great deal of money for Cohn's company.

Jules White was no Fritz Lang or Frank Capra, but nevertheless he was a master in his own field, the violence-prone comedy, and in 1982 he was given an award by the Academy of Motion Picture Arts and Science for his contribution to screen comedy. Jules White directed 104 Stooges films, whilst Del Lord made 39 and Ed Bernds 25. One single two-reeler was directed by Raymond McCarey – brother of the man who discovered Laurel and Hardy, Leo McCarey – and Clyde Bruckman (see the chapter on W. C. Fields).

In 1958, the year Harry Cohn died, the Short Subjects Department was closed. Jules White did not want to continue without Cohn and the new management of Columbia saw little future in the short film. The Stooges continued to make feature films, though, the last of which was *The Outlaws IS Coming* (1965). The reaction of the *New York Herald Tribune:* 'For Stooges buffs it ARE a lot of fun!'

When two of the original Stooges, Moe Howard and Larry Fine, both died in 1975, it was the end of a brand of comedy which is difficult to classify in any one cinematic genre. Slapstick, perhaps, but it had little in common with the kind of slapstick that came from the studios of Al Christie, Mack Sennett and Hal E. Roach. Nor can it really be called 'screwball' comedy. Really it stands in a class of its own: Stooges films. Amongst their vast *oeuvre,* with its many combinations of actors and directors, there are many which stand above the rest. The films were

The Three Stooges Go Around the World in a Daze (1963), loosely based on Jules Verne, with (left to right) Moe Howard, Joe DeRita and Larry Fine.

intended to warm up a cinema audience prior to the main feature: to be properly appreciated, they need to be viewed in the expectant atmosphere of a full cinema auditorium, more than likely with people squeezing noisily past you to get to their seats.

The titles of The Three Stooges' films have a special wit of their own. There were many parodies of existing film titles: *Nutty But Nice* (1940), from *Naughty But Nice* (1934). There were song titles, such as *Yes, We Have No Bonanza* (1939), inspired by the song 'Yes, We Have No Bananas'. 'Nuts to You' becomes the film *Mutts to You* (1938) and 'Read 'Em and Weep' becomes *Rhythm and Weep* (1946).

The Three Stooges' films are well-known throughout the world, and in countries where television is a major part of people's lives they are being brought to new audiences all the time. There is one exception: the Soviet Union. When a request came for some shorts to be shown in Russian cinemas in 1956, it was supposedly refused by the Americans on the grounds that 'They intended to use them to depict Americans being brutalized by eye-gouging, kicks in the shin and twisted noses, in the name of fun!' (*Whatever Became Of...* by Richard Lamparski, Bantam Books, New York, 1973).

Most film historians have quite rightly described The Three Stooges' contribution to the cinema as a large number of uncomplicated, well-made features and shorts. They are B-movies, but it would not be fair to call them 'pulp'. Sometimes they were made using superb art-deco scenery which had been left intact for a few days after the making of an A-film by someone else. Though few of the films took much time to make, they were unrehearsed and well-choreographed. They are bizarre examples of the Hollywood comedy of a bygone age: light, middle-of-the-road comedies which nevertheless deserve our attention. All were made with great expertise in every area of cinematography. This has given them a professionalism and entertainment value which is lacking from many of the most ambitious films being made today.

9

Martin and Lewis
(Dino and Jerry)

In the early 1950s, Jerry Lewis' wife, Patti, hung a sign on the front door of their house in St Cloud Road, Hollywood. It read: 'Jerry Lewis is not allowed in this house!'

It wasn't that there was anything wrong with their marriage (they married in 1944 and are still together), but the fact was that he had the habit of being a comedian at home as well as at work, and as far as his family was concerned he was a walking disaster area. He has sometimes said in interviews that he reacts almost instinctively to the spotlight being trained on him and being expected to be instantly funny, almost to the point where when he opens the refrigerator and the light comes on he launches into a twenty-minute comedy act.

This has always been the strength of Jerry Lewis: improvising, making the most of a situation, acting intuitively. This quality soon became apparent when, in 1946, he teamed up with Dean Martin as an entertainer in the Copacabana Club in New York. On 20 July of that year, Harold Brent Wallis (b. 1899), a film producer with Paramount, saw them for the first time, Hal B. Wallis was perplexed. Martin and Lewis combined physical attractiveness with zany verbal humour directed not only at each other but at the audience. They walked around the auditorium, helped themselves to people's drinks, and cut off men's ties. By the time this inanity reaches its climax, the audience was wildly enthusiastic. In 1978 Orson Welles told Peter Bogdanovich, in the magazine *Esquire,* that he had actually seen people literally wetting themselves during one of these acts by Martin and Lewis.

Hal B. Wallis describes his first meeting with the pair in his biography, *Starmaker* (1980): 'Dean, tall and handsome, didn't look like a comedian and Jerry, equipped with a mouthful of oversized false teeth and chimpanzee-like hairpiece, seemed grotesque!' Dean Martin

Dean Martin and Jerry Lewis on the set for *The Caddy* (1953).

was nineteen at the time, and Jerry twenty.

Wallis waited until they appeared at Slapsie Maxie's Club in Hollywood in the summer of 1948. Again, their act was pure, beautifully crafted chaos, more anarchic than the Marx Brothers and with the assault and battery of old-fashioned comedy brought right up to date. Their audiences were starting to include people from other film studios. Wallis arranged a screen test for Martin and Lewis in the studios at Paramount. The test confounded all his expectations, though: when Martin and Lewis went into an empty studio with someone else's script their charisma vanished and the act did not work at all. They tried a second screen test, which turned out just as badly on film: they were too tense, and their humour was woolly. Then Wallis suggested they do one of their ordinary comedy routines in front of the studio staff during one of the breaks. It was a brilliant success, and everyone loved it. Wallis had found the solution: don't keep Martin and Lewis strictly to a script, give them plenty of freedom of movement and allow them to play around, rehearse the act as little as possible. And so a new team of film comedians was born.

The question now was, what kind of films should they act in? Writer Cy Howard came up with the suggestion that they appear in *My Friend Irma* (1949), the cinema version of the CBS radio series of the same name, begun in 1947, in which Marie Wilson (1916-72) played a clichéd dumb blonde. The fact that the radio show was well-known and popular should make the public receptive to a film, and the risk of its being a flop because of the introduction of two unknown actors was reduced. *My Friend Irma* was a success. Martin and Lewis signed a seven-year contract under which they had to make one film a year for Paramount and would each receive $75,000 per film. Martin and Lewis also hastily set up their own York Pictures Corporation, a paper company one-third owned by Paramount for tax reasons, also to make one film a year which would be distributed by Paramount. This would ensure that there was a Martin and Lewis film showing in the cinemas during each summer and Christmas holiday. They would also continue to do live appearances and work for radio and TV. Their films would be made by such venerable comedy directors as George Marshall (1891-1975), who worked with Laurel and Hardy and W. C. Fields; Norman Taurog (b. 1899) who was making Larry Semon comedies as early as 1919; and Frank Tashlin (1913-72), an ex-cartoonist and Disney story editor as well as a gag-writer for Hal Roach. Jerry Lewis later said that it was Tashlin who taught him most of what he knew about films.

In the Martin and Lewis films, Dean Martin is the good-looking easy-going crooner who never has any trouble with the opposite sex. Jerry Lewis is a barrel full of contradictions, a well-nigh schizophrenic type, an awkward young man (but what a nice face) in a sweater, light blue trousers that are too short for him, white socks and trainers, who does everything possible to spoil Dean Martin's approaches to women and his self-assured passage through life. He is not an inherently comic person himself, in the way that Charlie Chaplin or Laurel and Hardy are: his humour comes from the art of imitation, and he is equally at home satirizing a gangster, pilot, professor, male nurse, trainee waiter, soldier or sailor or anything else. He has his own bizarre, inimitable style. Excluding the two 'Irma' films, *My Friend Irma* and *My Friend Irma Goes West* (their first film as a duo was actually *At War with the Army,* made in 1950), they made a total of fifteen films for Paramount. Their audience consisted predominantly of teenagers and children, who immediately took to their brand of humour. Almost as quickly, a large group of Martin-and-Lewis-Haters sprang up. You either love Dean and Jerry, or you hate them: there's no middle way.

In 1956 Dean Martin and Jerry Lewis went their own separate ways and the duo ceased to exist. On 25 July 1956, ten years after their first club appearance, they were billed as a worldwide attraction for the last time. Their last film was *Hollywood or Bust* (1956) and Dean Martin also left York Pictures Corporation.

When Jerry Lewis was a guest on NBC's 'Eddie Fisher Show' on 30 September 1958, he hinted that Dino (as Martin was called in America) and 'Jer' were planning to work together again. Jerry Lewis was about to sing when all of a sudden Dean Martin and Bing Crosby rushed onto the stage, shouting 'Don't sing! Don't sing!' Dean and Jerry immediately launched into a high-speed exchange of repartee, just as they always used to (Jerry, pointing to Dean: 'Who wants to work with that drunk?' Dean to Jerry: 'How can you look so clean and laugh so dirty?'). Crosby and Fisher were doubled up with laughter, and the audience watching at home was excited. The next day's newspapers eagerly heralded a comeback by Martin and Lewis. But they were jumping to conclusions: the comeback never took place.

For Dean Martin, who subsequently turned out to be a successful singer, popular television personality and a good film actor into the bargain, the period he spent as a singing straight man to Jerry Lewis became a thing of the past. It took a great deal of effort to rid himself of his image as one half of a comedy team, but he succeeded, helped by the clan that surrounded Frank Sinatra.

Dean Martin's original name was Dino Paul Crocetti. He comes from Steubenville, Ohio, known as Little Chicago because of its high crime rate. He was born on 17 June 1927, the son of the local barber, Guy Crocetti. He married three times: Elizabeth MacDonald in 1940, Jeanne Beiggers in 1949 and Catherine Mae Hawn in 1973. He has seven children, all of whom have made occasional appearances on his TV shows: Craig, Claudia, Gail, Deanna, Jeanne, Dino Junior and Ricci. He was Dino Martin when he introduced himself as a singer to Sammy Watkins' band, where he stayed for three years before going on to work on his own as an entertainer and vocalist in night clubs.

Before his début as a singer, Dean Martin's education had been a sporadic one, interrupted by periods of truancy, and he had also worked as a filling-station attendant, deliveryman for moonshine whisky and professional gambler. He also won several amateur boxing championships. Many of the older inhabitants of Steubenville still remember the dark, sports-mad and resourceful Dino.

Jerry Lewis' real name is Joseph Levitch. He first saw the light of day on 16 March, 1926, in Newark, New Jersey, the son of a Jewish artiste couple. In 1944 he married the singer in the Ted Rio Fito band, Patti Palmer. A year later his son, Gary, was born, but he was not an only child for long. Jerry and Patti adopted five sons: Ronald, Scott, Christopher, Anthony and Joseph. Jerry Lewis is mad about children: his friend, director Frank Tashlin, once said that this was because he had had such a sad, lonely childhood. His parents were always away 'touring', and Jerry would be left behind with friends and relatives. Only in the summer holidays would the Levitches take their son along with them for a few weeks. It was during these occasional happy days away from home that he was first attracted to show business, and he liked the trips to the Catskills with Rae and Danny Levitch.

He began his career as an entertainer at the age of sixteen, working as a kind of master of ceremonies in the Paramount Theater in New York City, where he was later to be so successful with Dean Martin. They actually met in 1946, when they were both appearing separately in a night club. Jerry had acted as babysitter for his older colleague on a few occasions. Dean was a kind of elder brother to Jerry, who was jealous of his good looks and expertise: it is quite possible that he felt inferior to Dean Martin. When Hal B. Wallis signed them up as a duo, Jerry initially refused to play the role of pleasant but stupid underdog whilst Dino was given the glamorous role. He protested vociferously, but Hal Wallis persevered, and eventually managed to persuade him that he should at least give the part a try. Once he realized how much the public liked it, he was happy, though his relationship with Paramount and Dean Martin was never perfect. Almost every day something irritated him about them, and less than a year after they became Paramount's resident comedians he was speaking to technicians, designers, editors and press as though it was he, and not Barney Balaban, who was boss of the company.

This imperious tone was a life-long trait, and it rubbed many people up the wrong way. Only one person was able to stand up to it: Dean Martin always seems to have been unmoved by his parner's whims. He always apparently found it highly amusing and played along with Jerry's attempts to give him more minor roles in their films.

At the end of 1953, Paramount hired the Clyde Beatty Circus, with all its people, animals and props, for $30,000 a week. The tent and caravans were to serve as the location for their film, *Three Ring Circus*. By now, Dean Martin had dispiritedly given up the struggle against the scheming Jerry Lewis. Jerry would no longer even accept that Dean Martin appeared first on the screen in any of their films: he wanted this privilege for himself. The couple were no longer on speaking terms away from the cameras. In interviews, Dean Martin said with unaccustomed cynicism of *Three Ring Circus:* 'All I get to do in this turkey is sing "It's a Big, Wide, Wonderful World" to an elephant!'

Children visiting the sets of their films (all their outside locations were open to the public) would rush up to Dean Martin and yell: 'Hey, where's Jerry?' Producer Hal Wallis was constantly forced to remake scenes because they were so bad. He spoke to his two top comedians as though they were children, which usually induced them to make barely acceptable comedy.

Another few films were made during this unpleasant state of affairs, until Jerry Lewis rang Hal Wallis in December 1956 and pleaded with him to be allowed to make films on his own. Wallis agreed, realizing that the way things were now, they were not going to be a profitable act for much longer. In fact, the contract between Paramount and Martin and Lewis signed in 1949 had now expired. Jerry Lewis' first solo films, *The Delicate Delinquent* (1957) and *The Sad Sack* (1958) were a success with young Martin and Lewis fans, who hardly noticed Dean Martin's absence. As a mark of gratitude for the opportunity he had been given, Jerry Lewis sent Hal Wallis a gold clock inscribed: 'Thanks, Mr Hal!'

If Jerry Lewis had been domineering and ambitious as one half of a comedy team with Paramount, once he had proved that he was able to hold his own as a solo comedian he started becoming insufferable. There were a number of people in the film industry who accused him of having delusions of grandeur and described him as an intolerable

Dean Martin and Jerry Lewis before they parted company.

personality with an excessively high opinion of himself. By the time it came to making *Boeing-Boeing* (1965), in which Tony Curtis attempts to take over the role of Dean Martin in a duo, his conduct was unacceptable to Paramount.

In the winter of 1964, producer Bill Gray hired a fashionable Paris restaurant for two days to do some indoor filming. A whole floor of the Plaza Athene Hotel had been reserved for Jerry. Around midnight he arrived, complete with seventy-five suitcases, a personal hairdresser, a costume consultant, a PR man and a stand-in. Once his baggage had been taken upstairs, he rang room service and ordered salami sandwiches. The hotel apologized and said they didn't have any. So he walked downstairs, had all his cases brought down, and went off to stay in the Ritz Hotel (they had no salami either, so he sent someone off to scour the streets of Paris until he found some).

A few days later, the crew was ready to begin rehearsals in the restaurant, which had been rebuilt as a set for *Boeing-Boeing*. But the star of the film was nowhere to be found. He had left Paris that very morning and was now sitting on his yacht in San Diego waiting for Paramount to contact him: there had been another disagreement with the studios over how much he was paid. For the time being, Paramount

The Sad Sack, the second film in which Jerry Lewis played without Dean Martin.

gave in to his whims, but it was Jerry Lewis' last picture for Paramount. His next, *Three on a Couch* (1966), was made by Columbia Pictures.

So far, Jerry Lewis has made twenty-five films without Dean Martin. In addition, he has appeared as a guest star in two films, *Li'l Abner* in 1959 and *It's a Mad, Mad, Mad, Mad World* in 1963. Eight of his solo films were directed by Frank Tashlin, and the rest were written, directed and edited by Lewis himself, assisted on the Moviola editing machine by Rusty Wiles. In 1970 Lewis directed a film starring Sammy Davis Jr and Peter Lawford, *One More Time,* not one of cinema's great masterpieces.

Dean Martin, in the meantime, was having a certain amount of success with his television shows, exploiting his 'ragamuffin' image and giving the impression that his performances in front of NBC's cameras were live. So, for example, he could nonchalantly light up a cigarette, eye up a chorus girl and drunkenly sing: 'It's June in January, 'cause I'm in Australia!' He is at his best in feature films (such as *Rio Grande* in 1959 and *Bandolero* in 1968), though he is also an excellent TV performer. Unlike his only two real competitors, Perry Como and Andy Williams, he makes old-fashioned live television. In *Time* magazine dated 11 March 1966, actor Anthony Quinn says of TV host, Dean Martin: 'All of us seem to be plagued by responsibility, hemmed in by convention. Dean is the symbol of the guy who can go on, get drunk, have no responsibilities!' And when Lucille Ball appeared as a guest on 'The Dean Martin Show' she said: 'You know Dino, you make cooked spaghetti look tense!'

Dean Martin still jokes about his former partner. For example, to Jerry Lewis' annoyance, for two whole seasons from 1967 to 1969, at which time Jerry Lewis also had his own TV show for NBC, Dean Martin would end his show with the words: 'Y'all watch "The Jerry Lewis Show" this Tuesday night, 'cause I will!'

Jerry Lewis opened a restaurant on Sunset Boulevard in Hollywood, with the initials JL on the doors and the cutlery. He became part owner of a cinema company, Jerry Lewis Mini Cinemas, showing only good family entertainment, and the company opened 750 small cinemas all over America. In 1979 it went bankrupt, which was partly the fault of the International Alliance of Theatrical Stage Employees and Moving Picture Operators of the United States. In America there is a union agreement that there will always be two projectionists belonging to the union present at every cinema performance. For a large chain, this can have a huge inflationary effect on wages costs.

Jerry Lewis' films have always made a great deal more in American box-office takings than they ever cost to make; likewise, the films he made with Dean Martin were reliable money-spinners. By the end of the sixties and in the early seventies, he was even being dubbed 'Le Roi du Crazy' by highbrow film magazines like *Positif* and *Les Cahiers du Cinéma*. In 1971 he performed in front of capacity audiences for sixteen nights at the Paris Olympia and his films were shown for weeks in the cinemas of the French capital. Lewis grew a beard and began giving

The Stooge (1951).

lessons on how to make films. To French *nouvelle vague* film enthusiasts and people in the industry he was regarded not as an 'irrepressible clown' as he was in the States, but as the prototype of the modern *auteur* film-maker who is involved in every stage of the making of the film. Jerry Lewis was indeed a producer, director, writer, actor/comedian, film and music editor all rolled into one: like any self-respecting artist, he did everything himself!

The French adored Jerry Lewis and he was swamped with invitations to teach the subject of film. His European admirers included such major figures as Jean-Luc Godard and François Truffaut. In a foreword to a book put together from hundreds of recordings made of workshops at the University of Southern California (Warner Books, New York,

94

Money From Home (1953).

1973), Godard says 'Jerry Lewis is the only American director who has made progressive films. He is much better than Chaplin or Keaton!'

It is certainly true that Jerry Lewis is experienced in many different areas of film-making, and as a technician too he is aware of what can and cannot be done, though in 1960 he was still getting into trouble with the sound technicians' and cameramen's unions. When he was making *The Bellboy* he decided not to use the boom microphones in the studio, but instead to experiment with small cordless microphones and directional microphones placed around the studio in strategic places. The boom operators contacted their union. Likewise when the cinematographers heard that he planned to set up a TV camera beside each film camera so that the shots could be monitored by the director. Rule No. 1 in American film- and TV-making is never to try and introduce new working methods: this is asking for trouble, and the unions will make you very much aware of their opinions.

Neverthelsss, Jerry Lewis was the first Hollywood director to use cordless microphones and to use TV cameras as monitors: both are now accepted methods of making a film and Lewis managed to overcome the resistance of the unions.

Hardly any Jerry Lewis films were made between 1970 and 1980. *Which Way to the Front* (1970) and *Hardly Working* (1979) were less successful than the average Martin and Lewis film of yesteryear. But Jerry Lewis managed to stay in the headlines, particularly as promoter and anchorman of the annual Muscular Dystrophy Labor Day Telethon which has raised millions of dollars for sufferers from the disease. It is something of a puzzle why he got involved with this particular charity, though it is known that from 1964 to 1979 he was physically and psychologically dependent on the painkiller Percodan which he took for a damaged vertebra which happened during a deliberate stage fall in one of his live appearances. It took an operation to relieve him finally of his discomfort. But this cannot be the reason for his preoccupation with the Telethons, and he never talks about the subject when interviewed.

During 1972 and 1973 Jerry Lewis began work on a French/Swedish co-production called *The Day the Clown Cried*, in which he directs himself in the role of a circus clown in the Second World War who is deported from Paris to a concentration camp. Here he continues to play the clown, but cracking his jokes as the children make their way to the gas chambers. He was a clown in hell.

In a *New York Sunday Times* interview in 1969, Jerry Lewis said: 'Comedy is a man in trouble.' In his book, *Total Film-Maker* (1973): 'I am nine years old when performing comedy. At that age, hurt is possible but degradation is seldom possible.' A nine-year-old boy: at that sort of age, adults will let you get away with a great deal.

A clown in hell indeed.

Sixteen years after the initial editing work was completed on *The Day the Clown Cried*, it has still never been shown in public. The master copy is lying in a vault somewhere and Jerry Lewis will not discuss it, though he has said that the public will get to see it one day.

In his second-to-last film, *Hardly Working*, Lewis again played a clown, just as he had in *The Family Jewels* in 1965. In 1979 it became clear that the public no longer had much time for a fifty-three-year-old comedian who acted like a young boy. At the beginning of the film there is a selection of old Jerry Lewis scenes, and this anthology is a good deal funnier than the film that follows it. Woody Allen, Mel Brooks, Monty Python and the National Lampoon team had taken over the genre of comedy by this time. What was more, reruns of Laurel and Hardy films were very popular in America and it was sometimes painfully obvious how much Jerry Lewis modelled himself on Stan Laurel.

In *Sailor Beware* (1951), for example, one of the best Martin and

'The Dean Martin Show'
(1965-74). Dean Martin's
gimmick in these shows was
pretending to be drunk.

Lewis comedies, Jerry Lewis takes part in a boxing match that is almost
identical to that of 'Smiling' Laurel in the two-reeler, *Any Old Port*,
made in 1932.

   They also play a brilliant scene in *Sailor Beware* in a dressing-room,
just before the boxing match. The opponent is sitting on a massage table
stripped to the waist; his assistant is a very young James Dean. Martin
and Lewis, playing sailors Hal and Melvin, have decided to launch a
psychological attack on the opponent to try to demoralize him. They
carry on a loud discussion designed to show that Melvin is a killer, a
fighting machine nothing and no one can withstand, a true professional.

   Whilst Dean Martin massages him, Jerry Lewis aggressively beats his fists together and pretends to have been brain-damaged by all his years in the ring. He is the typical veteran sportsman going round in a permanent daze. Sometimes, when he is unable to get his words out, Dean Martin will thump him on the head so that he resumes his speech like a record that was stuck.

Martin: What are you, a boxer?
Lewis: What do I look like, a cocker spaniel? I eh, I eh, I eh…
(Martin hits him hard)
Lewis: I was fighting Gene Tierney once, and…
Martin: You mean Gene Tunney!
Lewis: You fight who you want, I'll fight who I want!

So it goes on, but the opponent has been made so nervous by all this talk that he is replaced by an even stronger boxer. In *The Sad Sack* (1958), soldier Jerry Lewis absent-mindedly empties the contents of a tipper truck full of sand onto his sergeant's open jeep. Stan Laurel does exactly the same to Oliver Hardy and his convertible in *Blockheads*, twenty years earlier in 1938! It is possible that Jerry Lewis used Stan Laurel's gags legitimately: the two comedians often sat discussing the cinema in Stan's flat in Santa Monica, and Lewis was also on friendly terms with Chaplin, who at one time gave him a copy of *Modern Times* as a present. Certainly, whenever Jerry Lewis was asked who he thought were the best American film comedians, he would always reply: 'Chaplin and Stan Laurel, in that order!'

But Jerry Lewis' days as a film comedian were drawing to a close by the time he reached the age of sixty. It is possible that he might have gone on to preserve his high standards working as a director or scriptwriter, but he was becoming much less of a major figure in the cinema world, and people were starting to think of him again as half of the Martin and Lewis comedy team, or possibly as a slightly underestimated solo comedian. He made one more appearance in 1983 in a Martin Scorsese film, *The King of Comedy,* where he played a famous TV personality, Jerry Langford, constantly waylaid by the psychopathic Rupert Pupkin, brilliantly played by Robert de Niro. If this role proves to be his last appearance on the screen, it would be a fitting end to the career of a brilliant entertainer.

10

Buster Keaton: The poker face

Anyone sitting down to watch their first Buster Keaton film is probably in for a surprise. Here is a smooth-faced comedian with a boater on his head running blindly after women whilst everywhere he goes houses fall in ruins around his ears, ships are wrecked, and he climbs up and down the outside of trains and buses without a second thought. Keaton emerges unscathed from predicaments that would leave a mere mortal severely injured (though he did once break a leg whilst filming *The Electric House* in September 1921).

But perhaps Buster Keaton's most distinctive feature is the fact that during all these adventures and disasters his face never once betrays any expression. Whatever happens, he retains his poker-faced mien. He never laughs: sometimes in his gazelle-like eyes there is a glimmer of a smile, though it only shows up if you are seeing a 35mm film on a full-size cinema screen. He appears to have laughed on screen only twice in his entire career: once in *Fatty at Coney Island* (1917) and once at the end of the French film, *Le Roi des Champs-Elysées* (1934) just before he clasps the woman of his dreams in his arms. But these are exceptions that prove the rule: apart from never laughing on camera, he rarely did so in his private life either. In *The Ladies Home Journal* of June 1926, he explains in an article ('Why I never smile') that from very early on, as a child on the stage, he realized that people laughed at him, not with him. His father also cured him somewhat harshly of his habit of laughing in public.

Buster Keaton was born on 4 October 1895 and died on 1 February 1966. He was the oldest son of two knockabout entertainers, Joseph Hollie Keaton (1867-1946) and Myra Edith Cutler (1877-1955). He was born at a time when the Two Keatons were appearing in an act in Piqua, Kansas with the Mohawk Medicine Company, a colourful group of entertainers who travelled round fairs and circuses and sometimes also small theatres. He was not even six months old when his mother placed Joseph Francis Keaton in a trunk on the side of the stage so that she could keep an eye on him while she was working. As he grew up, he clambered all over everything; in 1896 he fell off a piece of scenery almost straight into the arms of 'Doc' Harry Houdini, who was another member of the troupe, which also functioned as a sales point for 'miracle cures' for various maladies. Houdini is supposed to have said to Keaton the Elder: 'That's some buster your baby took!', and from that moment he was called Buster Keaton. By the time he was three, he had insisted on becoming a member of the act, and the Two Keatons became the Three Keatons. He was made up, bewigged and dressed as a miniature replica of his father.

At this age, Buster Keaton was not so much a performer as a stage prop. He was unremittingly hurled around the stage and Mrs Keaton even sewed a handle onto his jacket so that she could swing him around more easily. Not infrequently his loving parents would throw him over the orchestra pit into the auditorium.

By the time he was five, Buster Keaton was a true professional who learned all the tricks of the trade simply by playing. His knowledge did not come from his father or other members of the variety group: he was entirely self-taught. He was constantly imitating the adults around him, the theatre was his whole world and he was used to having to clown around if he wanted to gain his parents' attention or sympathy. He spent precisely one morning at school: in the classroom he did exactly what his instructors told him to do, and regarded school as a stage

Sherlock, Jr. (1942), a silent
film in which Keaton plays a
projectionist who dreams of
becoming a detective.

appearance. The teacher sent him back to the boarding-house where his
parents were staying with a note: because of his lack of discipline and
poor concentration, he could stay away in future.

When Buster was six, it was his name which received star billing on
the posters for the show: 'The Three Keatons. Buster, assisted by Joe
and Myra!' At the age of nine, he was featured in *Billboard*, the trade
newspaper for the entertainment business, as 'Buster Keaton,
Acknowledged to be the Best Comedian of his Age and Inches on the
Stage!'

His father Joe was beginning to make more and more appearances on
the stage in a state of inebriation, which put the lives of the other two
members of the acrobatic trio in danger. In 1917, Buster was able to
escape all this: impresario Max Hart got him a job as a comedian at the
Winter Garden in New York, playing in *The Passing Show of 1918* for
$250 a week. The show was run by the brothers Lee and Jacob Shubert,
two major figures in the world of vauderville at the time (their
descendants still own chains of theatres in the United States).

But a day before rehearsals began, Buster Keaton met an old friend,
the 'Dutch' comedian Lou Anger, who introduced him to Roscoe
'Fatty' Arbuckle (1887-1933), an extremely corpulent film comedian
who had just left Mack Sennett's Keystone Company after making well
over a hundred shorts, and had now set up on his own as the Comique
Film Company. Arbuckle asked Keaton to appear in his latest two-
reeler, *The Butcher Boy* and took him on for $40 a week. Hart was

gracious about Keaton's contract with him having been broken: despite his membership of the then all-important Vauderville Managers' Association (an organization which was very important for any comedian to have on his side) he said that Buster Keaton had made a sensible decision. Although Keaton was losing $210 a week as a result, the 'high summer' of comedy was fast approaching.

Between 1917 and 1919, interrupted by six months' military service in France, Keaton made between fourteen and twenty short comedies with Arbuckle. The exact number of films is not known; nor are their titles. Arbuckle and Keaton took turns to direct the films: when Arbuckle was being filmed, Keaton would be behind the cameras; if Buster were acting, it would be Roscoe giving him directions. These two-reelers were made in a small studio on West 48th Street in New York, and later in a slightly larger one on 17th Street and on location at Long Beach. Buster Keaton and Roscoe Arbuckle formed a lasting friendship, and Buster always insisted in interviews that 'I learned it all from him.'

Both Jack Warner and William Fox offered Buster Keaton $1000 a week to go and work for them. He declined and elected to stay with Arbuckle. But Roscoe himself was about to leave the Comique Company and work with Zukor, so Buster accepted a suggestion from his future brother-in-law, Joseph Schenk, that Shenk set up a studio for him in what was formerly Charlie Chaplin's first studio. Metro-Goldwyn-Mayer were to distribute the films he made.

Roscoe 'Fatty, Arbuckle, Keaton's first film part was in one of Arbuckle's films, *The Butcher Boy* (1917) and the two were friends until Arbuckle's death in 1933.

In two years, Buster Keaton made nineteen two-reelers, fulfilling the roles of scriptwriter, gag-man, director, actor and editor all himself. He used the new medium of film as though it had been around for centuries. With editor J. Sherman Kell, he edited the films not on a Moviola machine or a cutting-table, but by hand, holding them up shot-by-shot against a light table and splicing them. Between 1917 and 1929 Buster Keaton churned out silent films twenty-four hours a day: to be precise, approximately thirty shorts and twelve features were made for the new Comique Company under Joseph M. Schenk, and in the first year with MGM. This twelve-year period produced his best work, including such films as *One Week* (1920), *The Navigator* (1924), *Go West* (1925), *Battling Butler* (1926), *The Cameraman* (1928) and *Spite Marriage* (1929).

Buster Keaton was the acrobatic comedian *par excellence*, a comedian with complete mastery of the 'pratfall' who retained his gimmick of appearing stony-faced right to the end of his career. Because of the ballet-like nature of his acrobatics and the breathtaking stunts he always insisted on performing himself, he was called the Fred Astaire of slapstick. But he was not a banana-skin or custard-pie comedian: he had his own, unique style which no one else in the business was ever able to imitate. Charles Chaplin was imitated by people like Billy West, Harold Lloyd by John Hines and Douglas Maclean, and Harry Langdon by Lloyd Hamilton, but in Buster Keaton's case they never bothered even trying. And this was in a world where it was not considered particularly reprehensible to borrow from someone else's repertoire. Keaton's gags do crop up in other people's films, though: in 1950, Jack Donoghue directed Red Skelton in *Watch the Birdie* for MGM. This was almost a remake of Keaton's *The Cameraman* of 1928. Theatre, film and TV writer Max Wilk says in his book, *Every Day's a Matinée* (Norton, New York, 1975): 'If you've never seen Mr Keaton in *The Cameraman*, then you can't know where Red Skelton got all his routines twenty years later in *Watch the Birdie*!'

Keaton was also the most silent of the silent comedians. Silent comedy is a totally separate medium, in a class of its own, and there are still fans who lament the fact that the talkie originated from silent film: it should have been the other way round.

If some of Chaplin's films, particularly the older two-reelers, seem very dated and old-fashioned today, it is much less true of Keaton's films. Most seem just as up-to-date as when they were first released. *The Cameraman*, made in 1928, seems just as brilliant as it always was, and after a few minutes the viewer forgets that this was made nearly sixty years ago. One MGM employee said, in the *Motion Picture Herald* in 1959, that *The Cameraman* had been used for years by the studio as a training film for new members of MGM's stock company.

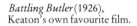

Battling Butler (1926), Keaton's own favourite film.

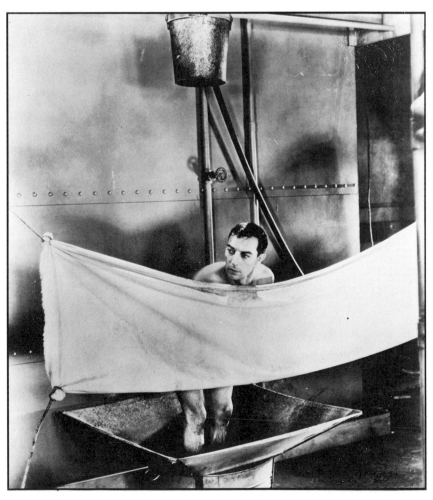

The bunglings of street photographer, Luke Shannon, who photographs a girl working in a film studio (Sally), takes her a copy of the photograph and then tries to win her love and respect by working as a news cameraman, is both funny and moving. The story was written by Clyde Bruckman, who later shot himself through the head after a meal in a Hollywood restaurant in 1953, using a revolver borrowed from Buster Keaton. It still retains as much fascination as ever; so do most of the films Keaton made between 1919 and 1929. In *Sherlock, Jr,* Buster is a cinema projectionist with aspirations towards working as a detective. Eventually he decides to take part in the film he is screening at the time, and walks straight through the screen into the film. This involved trick photography (by Fred Gabourie and Buster Keaton) which was very advanced for its time. The script was again by the unfortunate Clyde Bruckman, who Keaton greatly enjoyed working with. In *The General,* a multiple-reel feature made in 1926, Johnnie Gray (Buster Keaton) becomes entangled in the war between North and South. The film is a work of genius, showing how Keaton manages to save Annabelle Lee (Marian Mack) and a locomotive (his two great loves). The film is generally considered to be Keaton's masterpiece, and has been described and analysed in countless books.

One thing Buster Keaton did lack, compared to the two other great Hollywood silent comedians, Charles Chaplin and Harold Lloyd, was business acumen. He never owned the rights to his films in the way that Chaplin and Lloyd did, and they both eventually went on to produce their own films and therefore acquire the rights automatically. In 1928 this poor business sense on Keaton's part led to the greatest mistake of his career. Urged to do so by his brother-in-law, Joe Schenk (who was married to Norma Talmadge, the sister of Keaton's first wife, Natalie Talmadge), Keaton went to work for MGM. Schenk persuaded Keaton

Day Dreams (1922). No complete copies of this film exist now.

to do so because his brother, Nicholas Schenk, was one of the leading lights of MGM, and the company was very much aware of how much capital there was to be made from Keaton. In the book, *My Wonderful World of Slapstick* (Doubleday, New York, 1960), Keaton said to Charles Samuels, 'I made the worst mistake of my career. Against my better judgement I let Joe Schenk talk me into giving up my own studio to make pictures at the booming MGM lot in Culver City!'

MGM was very much a film-factory. It was high-pressure work, more impersonal than Keaton's own studio, with little eye for detail or for a good gag. When he made his first feature film for MGM, *The Cameraman*, Keaton still had old friends to work with, such as Clyde Bruckman, who wrote the script, cameramen Elgin Lessley and Reggie Lanning, technical adviser Fred Gabourie (who had worked on *Sherlock, Jr*, amongst other films), and director Edward Sedgwick, whom Buster had known since his early days in vaudeville when he was one of the Five Sedgwicks appearing in the same 'medicine shows' as The Three Keatons.

The Cameraman was the only really good film Keaton made with MGM, despite his salary of $150,000 a year. None of those he made subsequently attain the same level of his previous films, and from now on his career was to be a steady downhill progression.

At almost the same age as his father, Keaton acquired a liking for the bottle. He was becoming frustrated that he could not work in the way he was used to, and his alcoholism meant that he had little or no interest in the final results of his film-making. He had two sons from his first marriage to Natalie Talmadge: James (Jimmy) was born in June 1922, and Robert (Bobby) in February 1924. He was totally devoted to his sons and was brought even closer to them by the problems with the marriage. In 1933, he married the woman who had nursed him in a clinic for alcoholics, Mae Scribbens, who had also helped comedian Joe E. Brown to combat his dependence on drink. His third marriage was in 1940, to the woman who stayed with him until he died: Eleanor Norris. Six years previously, in 1934, his contract with MGM ran out and he was out of a job. But this was short-lived: he went to work for the low-budget Educational Studios, a refuge for new talent and for talent that was on the way back in. Here, between 1934 and 1937, he made sixteen two-reelers, none of them reaching his previous standard as his addiction to alcohol continued to plague him. In one of the comedies he made for Educational, *Palooka from Paducah*, his father Joe, mother Myra and sister Louise appear alongside him, whilst in *Nest on Wheels* his brother Harry and sister Louise both play parts. In October 1935, no less distinguished a person than the King of Silent Comedy, Mack Sennett, directed Keaton in another two-reeler for Educational, *The Timid Young Man*.

In 1939 Columbia welcomed Keaton with open arms, and it was here that he met Clyde Bruckman once again and worked for Jules White, the specialist in short comedies (see the chapter on The Three Stooges). In two years, White directed eight Keaton shorts.

Sergeant Deadhead (1965).
Left to right: Eve Arden,
Buster Keaton and Fred
Clark.

In the early forties, Keaton was back at MGM in Culver City, where he worked as a 'comedy constructionist' and gag-man for the princely sum of $100 a week. His job involved conceiving and writing scripts for comedians such as Red Skelton, the Marx Brothers, Mickey Rooney, Judy Garland and Laurel and Hardy. He also did similar work for Universal, but never received any screen credit for either. Eventually, MGM increased his salary to $300 a week.

Although it was starting to look very much as though Keaton's career was at an end, he remained in many different fields of film and broadcasting. In 1950 he guested on his fellow comedian Ed Wynn's TV show, and in the same year Garry Moore offered him a contract as a regular comedian on 'The Garry Moore Show'. After playing minor roles in the same way he had done with his parents in the vaudeville show, he began his own 'The Buster Keaton Show' for KTTV, a local TV station in Hollywood. With the help of his old friend Clyde Bruckman as writer and director, it was hailed as pure 'vaudeo' and was very successful, mainly amongst the inhabitants of the world's premier cinema city.

In 1952, 'Life With Buster' reached a wider public. His comedies from the 1930s were shown, sometimes cut, and in no particular order, under the heading 'The misadventures of Buster Keaton, a man struggling to cope with life's numerous problems.'

Many articles were written about Buster Keaton's films, including a piece by James Agee in *Life* magazine: 'Comedy's Greatest Era'. Buster was invited to appear on countless TV programmes: 'The James Melton

Show', 'The Twilight Zone', 'The Red Skelton Show', 'What's My Line?', 'The Donna Reed Show', 'Route 66', 'The Ed Sullivan Show' and many others. He made TV commercials, for Simon Pure Beer and other products, and appeared live in the Médrano Circus in Paris. He played major and minor roles in all kinds of American and foreign films, including his legendary appearance in *Limelight* with Charles Chaplin in 1952, where he played a very moving role as an ageing piano accompanist. He also worked with Samuel Beckett, who was living in Paris at the time, and the American director Alan Schneider, for whom he made a twenty-two-minute film, written by Beckett, called *Film – Esse Est Percipi* (To be is to be looked at). *Film* is a black-and-white two-reeler in the traditional 3:3 ratio, and it is still shown occasionally in Keaton retrospectives. In it, a man with a cloth over his face goes into a house, watched by a few passers-by. Inside, he closes the curtains, covers the bird cage and the fish tank, puts the dog and some cats out of the door, barricades the door, tears up photographs. Keaton, playing the man, can only be seen from behind. When we eventually see him from the front, his face bears a frightened and frightening expression: he is looking at his own face in the mirror. It is very much a film with a message. Originally, Beckett and Schneider had approached Charles Chaplin to play the role, but he was unavailable. Actor Jack MacGowan, who had appeared in plays by Beckett, was considered, but he cried off. It was not until this point that Beckett suggested Buster Keaton, whose films he especially liked. Keaton himself was not exactly awash with excitement about doing the film. In a postscript to the script

An episode of the CBS series 'Route 66' in which Buster Keaton (right) and comedian Joe E. Brown (left) guested. The actress is Jennie Maxwell.

of *Film,* Alan Schneider says that when he visited Keaton in Los Angeles, 'Buster thought Beckett and I were idiots. He accepted the offer because he needed the money. He came up with suggestions for improvements to the script because he didn't find the story funny. I told Buster that normally Beckett's writing didn't get improved or changed because Beckett wanted it to remain as it was written. Buster took me into his confidence: he had made a lot of films and there was no way any film longer than five minutes could be made from this script. He wanted to be paid to change the film and add some of his own ideas.'

If Schneider had agreed to Buster Keaton's suggestions, *Film* might have been rather more watchable. It was not received particularly well at the Venice Film Festival of 1965, where people were not entirely sure what to make of it. But the simple fact that Keaton was in it was enough to get him a standing ovation. The great master of film comedy, second only to Chaplin, was being praised by the press and the industry for all his old films. As he said to journalist Lotte Eisner over the applause: 'Sure it's great, but it's all thirty years too late!'

The film made by Beckett and Schneider shows a man who is a stranger to the outside world, who locks himself away from reality and is terrified by his own face in the mirror. Fortunately, it bore no resemblence to the real Buster Keaton, who was immersed in the business right up until his death: there was very little peace and quiet in his life. In 1957 Donald O'Connor played him in *The Buster Keaton Story,* and Robert Youngson's compilations such as *30 Years of Fun* (1962) and *Four Clowns* (1969) showed fragments of such films as *Cops, Day Dreams, The Balloonatic* and *Seven Chances* which had not been seen in cinemas for years. A book of blow-ups of stills from *The General* (1926) was also published. His films are now available on video and are still shown frequently on television.

In 'Once Upon a Time', an episode of 'The Twilight Zone' first shown by CBS on 15 December 1961, Buster Keaton plays Woodrow Mulligan, the assistant to Professor Gilbert, played by Milton Parsons. Keaton is transported forwards in time from 1890 to 1962. His face its usual inexpressive mask, Keaton wanders bewildered around this world of the future: it is a role that suits him perfectly. It is the same Keaton we see in his great films of the 1920s: one of life's great fictional misfits, the man who will always remain a stranger to the age in which he lives.

11
Charlie Chaplin: A legend

Charlie Chaplin, or rather Sir Charles Spencer Chaplin. Is there anything new still remaining to be written about him? Chaplin has received more attention than any other person in the history of cinema: comprehensive biographies, thick books of photographs and countless articles. This torrent of written and photographic material was added to a few years ago by a TV documentary made for Thames TV by film

historians Kevin Brownlow and David Gill: 'The Unknown Chaplin'.
This programme, consisting mainly of scenes rejected by Chaplin which
everyone thought had been thrown away, could well have marked the
end of the dissections of Chaplin's life and work both on paper and on
film. But in 1985 another book appeared, 800 pages long, describing
itself as the definitive biography of The Tramp: *Chaplin – His Life and
Art*. Whether it is definitive or not can be discovered only by half a
lifetime pottering around in archives, watching all the films he made at
least twice, and reading all the sixty or so other books which have been
written about him.

Chaplin died aged eighty-eight on 25 December 1977, in Corsier-
sur-Vevey on Lake Geneva, his wife Oona and seven of his eight
children sitting with him around the Christmas tree. Immediately,
magazine editors republished all the articles they had originally written
for his seventy-fifth and eightieth birthdays, describing him as Chaplin
the Tramp, Chaplin the Mysterious Genius, Chaplin the Lover of
Women, Chaplin the pure Film-Maker and Chaplin the Knower of
Men's Hearts. And in the years that followed his death, the printing
presses were never silent. More people wrote biographies to add to the
many that had already been published, from *Das Grosse Charlie
Chaplin Buch* to *The Great Charles Chaplin*. Most were illustrated
with stills, some instantly recognizable and some less well known. The
advent of video meant that the average consumer could build up their
own collection of shorts and feature films made by Chaplin or any other
comedian that took their fancy, and in fact it was probably video that
made books of stills from the films somewhat surplus to requirements.

The moving image now has so much more appeal to many people,
that if you want a book on Chaplin you will often have to order it
specially because they are such slow-moving items of stock as far as
booksellers are concerned. And yet Charles Chaplin is one of the best-
known and most popular film actors of all time.

During the ten years since his death, interest in Chaplin's films has
grown faster than ever before. When they are shown on television they
are not necessarily guaranteed to have the viewer laughing out loud,
possibly because (as we have stated earlier on in this book) when you
are watching television you are unlikely to be surrounded by a noisy,
expectant crowd of people. On the other hand, even in a full auditorium
some of his earlier Keystone, Essanay, Mutual and First National films
made betwen 1914 and 1917 can themselves leave a stony silence. Ask
any ten people and five will confess to loving Laurel and Hardy or even
Harold Lloyd films, but true Chaplin fans are thin on the ground.
Everyone will tell you what a great comedian he was, but few will drag
themselves out to their local independent cinema on a winter's night to
watch *The Gold Rush* (1952) or *The Great Dictator* (1940).

We can see from all the books, and of course from the films
themselves, how much Chaplin took pains to ensure that his comedies
were perfect in every way: comedy *is* a serious business, after all.
According to the Thames documentary, 'The Unknown Chaplin', his

quest for the perfect film sometimes led him to do dozens of retakes of a scene. Many ordinary people would have lost patience long before the tenth retake and decided to leave the scene as it stood, but Chaplin's perfectionism was one of the many marks of his genius.

The high point of 'The Unknown Chaplin' is the original opening scene of *City Lights* (1931), in which Chaplin stands in front of a corner-shop window and tries to use his walking stick to pry a piece of wood from between the bars of a grating set in the pavement. This magnificent sequence lasts more than five minutes. It is at times like this that one can see how right Dick Van Dyke was when he told *TV Guide* in 1969 that when you watch Chaplin, you are struck by his superb technique, and when you watch Stan Laurel it makes you laugh because it appears to happen by itself.

Even more interesting than 'The Unknown Chaplin' for anyone less familiar with Chaplin's work is a documentary film made in 1976 by Richard Patterson: *The Gentleman Tramp*. In this film, scenes from Chaplin's films are shown together with incidents from his life. In the case of many actors and actresses this technique would not work, because there is such a wide gap between the personalities they play on the screen and their own private lives. But in Chaplin's case, the two are very much bound up together, with Chaplin's personality constantly showing through in his films, and Patterson's technique gives us a powerful insight into the man and his work. The inter-cutting of documentary material on the public scandal that followed his paternity suit in the 1940s, complete with hate letters from American women's organizations, with the cynical scenes from his film *Monsieur Verdoux* (1947) where Chaplin plays a mass murderer, is particularly telling. A news item about the death when only three days old of the baby born after Chaplin's first marriage in 1919 was followed by a cradle scene from *The Kid* (1920). It is a sentimental scene, like most of Chaplin's films. The final scene of the documentary, referring to the last words Chaplin ever uttered in public ('Well, I have gone through a lot!') is just like the closing scene of *Modern Times* (1936). At the age of eighty-six Chaplin, leaning heavily on his wife Oona O'Neill's arm, shuffles round the garden of his house in Switzerland, the Manoir de Ban, and then out of the picture: the scene is perhaps even more evocative than the original end of *Modern Times*.

And what else is there that can be said about Chaplin's life? That the shoes he ate in *The Gold Rush* (1924) were made of liquorice; that the first Chaplin comedy ever to be shown on TV was broadcast by the DeForest Radio Corporation W2XCD in Passaic, New Jersey, on 9 March 1931; that the act with the bread rolls dancing around on a table with forks in them was copied from Roscoe Arbuckle; that he first appeared in his famous tramp's outfit when Mack Sennett told him to turn up in 'funny clothes' for the filming of *Kid Auto Races at Venice* (1914) and he helped himself to some clothes that were lying around Fatty Arbuckle and Chester Conklin's dressing-rooms? There is plenty of trivia surrounding Chaplin's life, though ultimately it is less interesting than his biography.

He was born on 16 April 1889 in a shabby flat in East Lane, Walworth, in South London. He was the second son of variety actress Hannah Hill, who worked under the stage name of Lilian Harley, and her second husband, Charles Chaplin the elder, who was a baritone with an unhealthy predilection for drink.

Chaplin's early years were positively Dickensian: he was surrounded by poverty and misery. His father literally drank himself to death: he died of alcoholic poisoning in St Thomas's Hospital in London in 1897. By the age of five young Charles was standing in for his mother on the stage in Croydon, as a singer, and at the age of ten he made his London début in a play at the Hippodrome. When he was seventeen, he joined the entertainment companies set up by Fred Wescott (1866-1941), Fred Karno's Companies and Fred Karno's Speechless Comedians, which between them had twenty groups of artistes touring music halls in England, North and South America, and Africa. It was with Fred Karno that Chaplin learned all the intricacies of show business and the qualities, such as high-class pantomine acting and perfect timing, that were to stand him in such good stead in his film career.

Top: *The Gold Rush* (1925), one of Chaplin's greatest films. Bottom: *The Circus* (1928). Charles Chaplin, with Henry Bergman in the background.

Another member of the Karno group who was just as talented as
Chaplin was Stanley Jefferson, later Stan Laurel. Chaplin and Jefferson
were the two major attractions on the bill, as well as being the director's
favourite performers. The two often worked together, and whilst
touring America with 'A Night in an English Music Hall' in 1910, they
even shared a room for a while. Although both came from similar
backgrounds and were only a year apart in age, there was never any
close contact between them once their attempts to seek their fortunes
in the United States had been successful. Stan Laurel did try to get in
touch with his former room-mate, but Chaplin never replied to his
letters. When he wrote *My Autobiography* (1964, New York), he made
no reference to Stan Laurel, though he does say of a photo of a hockey
team in which they both played whilst working for Fred Karno, 'Stan
Laurel is behind me.' With hindsight, it is possible that his refusal to
have anything to do with his compatriot and fellow comedian was a
mixture of fear and jealousy. Of all the comics who imitated Chaplin,
such as Harold Lloyd (with his Lonesome Luke), the Frenchman Max
Linder, the Mexican Charles Amador (who even had himself billed as

Chaplin with cameraman
'Rollie' Totheroh.

Charles Aplin), Billy West and Billie Ritchie, Stan Laurel was the only one who could imitate him perfectly. Even the professionals in the Fred Karno troupe sometimes failed to notice that Stan was standing in for Chaplin in one of their sketches. So Laurel did represent a potential threat to Chaplin. Laurel always spoke of him with admiration, though, and he recalls their trip together as Karno comedians from Britain to America on the S.S. *Cairnrona*, a tattered boat that was low on both comfort and stability. When land was finally sighted in mid-September 1910, said Stan to his biographer John McCabe sixty years later, everyone stood at the ship's rail and cheered. Chaplin took off his hat and cried, half seriously, 'America, I am coming to conquer you! Every man, woman and child shall have my name on their lips – Charles Spencer Chaplin!' The response of his fellow artistes was to hoot at him jokingly: 'Good Old Charlie!'

Once in America, Charles Chaplin worked in succession for Mack Sennett's Keystone studio (1914), Essanay (1915), Mutual (1916-17) and First National (1917-18). Sennett paid him $150 a week, Essanay $1250 a week. Mutual paid him an annual salary of $670,000 and First

A Night at the Show (1915): Chaplin and May White.

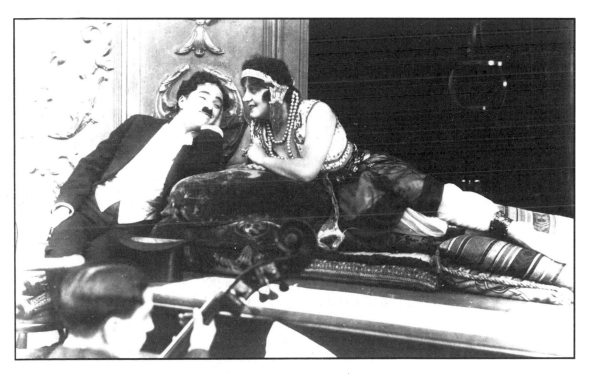

National gave him more than a million dollars for eight two-reelers. In October 1917 he opened his own Chaplin Studios on the corner of La Brea Avenue and Sunset Boulevard in Hollywood. On 17 April 1919 Charles Chaplin, Mary Pickford, Douglas Fairbanks and D. W. Griffith set up their own film production and distribution company, United Artists. Its headquarters was at 729 Seventh Avenue in New York; it was to have had a fifth member, film cowboy William S. Hart, but in the event he went to Paramount instead. The intention was for the

Work (1915). Chaplin with Edna Purviance, his leading lady in thirty-five films.

company to make and distribute three films a year, but in practice this was not to happen, for all sorts of reasons.

During the period when Chaplin was leaving Fred Karno's theatrical agency and moving to Keystone Studios, cinema was a medium which American intellectuals looked down on; it was seen as a simple amusement for Joe Public, and for the better sort of people, culture was a concert or a museum. Chaplin was not the first to bring comedy to the silver screen, or the first stage artist to move to cinema. When he made his first film (*Making a Living,* 1914) there was a ten-year-old tradition of film comedy in Europe. Many comedies were made in Italy around the turn of the century, and in England, Arthur Melbourne-Cooper was producing large volumes of cops-and-robbers films as early as 1898. In the United States, Mack Sennett and his staff had already established a following for films by the French comedian Max Linder and the Italians Fernando Guillaume (Polidor) and André Chapuis (Cretinetti).

One of Chaplin's major influences on the world of comedy from the outset was the fact that he slowed it down from its somewhat frenetic pace and introduced pantomine acting to it. After *Kid Auto Races at Venice,* his second film for Sennett, his future as a film comedian was assured. The Crystal Theater on 14th Street played Chaplin films continuously from 1915 to 1923, with one interruption of a few days to give them a chance to try showing someone else's. During that week, business was so slow that they went back to Chaplin films straight

115

afterwards. When Chaplin paid a short visit to London in 1921, he received more than 73,000 fan letters: the fairytale story of the Cockney lad made good in Hollywood captured the public imagination. The boy from the slums was soon a millionaire rubbing shoulders with people like Einstein, Toscanini, Chou En-Lai, Shaw, Cocteau, Churchill, Sartre, Picasso and Gandhi. His estate was valued at more than £500 million after he died.

Chaplin received an Academy Award in 1929 'for versatility and genius in writing, acting, directing and producing *The Circus*'. On 27 June 1962 Chaplin was awarded an honorary doctorate by Oxford

Chaplin masks were worn for the Dutch gala première of *Modern Times* (1936) in Amsterdam.

University, and in 1972 he received an Oscar when he returned to America after twenty years' absence, 'For the incalculable effect he has had on making motion pictures the art form of this century.' The presentation to Chaplin was the high point of the ceremony, not least because the American film industry was running the risk of Charlie dying before he had been thus honoured. Then, on 2 January 1975, Chaplin received a knighthood from the Queen.

Even during his lifetime the genius of Charles Spencer Chaplin in the art of film had become a legend. Nowadays, people watch his films with a mixture of wonder and admiration, but at the time when Chaplin was at the pinnacle of his career in silent films, as producer, director and actor, the world was a very different one. His audience in America consisted for the most part of large numbers of European immigrants and their descendants. Everyday life was often joyless: ordinary people had to contend with unemployment, corruption, a strict government and an élitist upper class. In the little tramp they saw in the cinema, they had an ally and a friend. When they saw waiters, barbers, students or policemen on the screen, it was the day-to-day reality they were used to, and the effect was a comic one. Chaplin used his abilities as a mime artist and acrobat to the full, but perhaps more importantly he was a great actor who could make use of the sentiments and emotions of his audience. He would often return, years later, to an idea he had dreamt up but not used, or which deserved to have more made out of it than he had previously. He guarded his copyrights with an almost neurotic fanaticism.

Chaplin owned the rights to all his United Artists films, but not those for his 35 Keystone films, 15 Essanay, 12 Mutual and 8 First National. In 1918 he acquired the right to the First National comedies, but those he had made for Keystone, Essanay and Mutual mostly became public-domain films and often appear on TV or video under titles different to their original ones, sometimes in cut form. The filmography at the end of this book gives the alternative names for his films.

As the documentary 'The Unknown Chaplin' showed, he is less unknown as far as his methods of working are concerned. From the books and articles that have been written about him since 1920, it is noticeable that every Chaplin movie is a kind of homage to Chaplin himself. His cameraman, Rolland H. Totheroh (1890-1967), who was working in Sennett's Keystone studios when Chaplin first arrived, worked for him for nearly thirty-five years. 'Rollie' filmed every movie Chaplin made from 1915 to *Monsieur Verdoux* in 1947. Chaplin did not want anyone else behind the camera and paid Totheroh very well. For his part, Totheroh did things exactly the way Chaplin wanted him to: the boss was always in the middle of the picture with the other actors circling round him. This was a rule that the faithful cameraman and his assistants always adhered to, much to Chaplin's satisfaction. If Totheroh had written his memoirs, who knows what fascinating details of his employer's techniques would now be public knowledge. Certainly, the two must have known each other very well, and yet in Chaplin's own autobiography there is not a single mention of him by name; nor is there a photo of the man who played such an important part in the history of the cinema. In *Film Culture* for spring 1972, there is a revealing comment in an interview with Totheroh about Chaplin's book. 'A lot of Charlie's autobiography to me is false, because I knew him so well. He's building himself up for a pinnacle I don't think he ever reached. As a genius, yes; he *is* a genius. He can talk on pretty near any subject. But if a person was really educated on the subject he was talking on, they'd see the errors he made. He always figures his masses, his public, no matter what he does, "Oh, they'll think it's great!"'

Chaplin preferred to do everything on his own in his profession as film-maker. He would brook no disagreement by others and reserved the right to dismiss actors and actresses, replace them with others and then in turn send the replacements home and bring the original cast back onto the set. When he directed films, he used a script or at the very least an outline, but this did not mean he felt constrained to stick to it all the time, as Hitchcock did. Particularly with the one- and two-reelers it would appear that Chaplin improvised a lot as he went along. This flexible method of film-making always resulted in something good eventually. Just like a novelist who will sometimes spend days on end waiting for inspiration to strike, and meanwhile sit moping behind the typewriter with a sheet of blank paper in it, so would Chaplin sometimes pace up and down the studio for days without a single yard of film being made. But the crew had to remain on constant alert, for eventually the moment of inspiration would come.

If Chaplin had been able to operate the camera while he acted, he would have done so. It is common knowledge that Chaplin's dislike of sound movies was because he had to put up with sound technicians on the floor of the studio giving him advice.

But even a lone wolf like Chaplin could not manage without other people's specialized knowledge. Whether he really was the composer of the legendary soundtrack to *Modern Times,* which includes 'Smile' and 'The Toy Waltz', is still open to doubt. David Raskin (b.1922), who

The Great Dictator (1940).
Chaplin is seen here with his
third wife, Paulette Goddard.
He plays both the shy
hairdresser and the dictator
Adenoid Hynkel.

wrote the music for at least sixty feature films from 1944 onwards and
was both conducting a major orchestra and playing in Benny
Goodman's orchestra at the age of fifteen, was asked to help Chaplin
with the music for *Modern Times* in 1936. In his book, *Music for the
Movies* (Cranbury, New York, 1973), Tony Thomas says: 'Raskin's job
was to make musical logic from the humming and whistling of
Chaplin!' After ten days, Chaplin removed Raskin from his job because
the two of them were not getting on together. Raskin had been
recommended to Chaplin by composer Alfred Newman, a famous
name in the music world. When Chaplin showed Newman the written
music that had resulted from his own whistling and humming,
Newman simply said it was a good piece of work by his young
colleague. Chaplin did what he often did: summoned the dismissed
composer back to the studio, increased his salary and allowed him the
privilege of listening to his humming for the next five months. A great
many back-room musicians were responsible for the soundtracks of
Chaplin's films; likewise his autobiography was edited by the
publishers from spoken tapes he made. So the idea of Chaplin doing
everything for himself is often a long way from the truth.

Charles Chaplin married four times. He married Mildred Harris in
1918, followed by Lita Grey in 1924, Paulette Goddard in 1936, and

A scene from *The Great Dictator* (1940). Left to right: Henry Daniell as Dr Garbitsch, Chaplin as Adenoid Hynkel and Jack Oakie as Benzino Napaloni.

Oona O'Neill in 1943. Altogether he had eight children: Geraldine, Michael-John, Josephine, Victoria, Eugene, Jane, Annette and Christopher. Oona O'Neill, the daughter of playwright Eugene O'Neill, was eighteen when she married the fifty-four-year-old comedian. It was an ill-kept secret that Chaplin had a predilection for young girls and he is also known to have consorted with various older women. At the end of 1943 he was involved in a lawsuit because of a daughter supposedly born from a liaison between himself and Joan Barry. Chaplin was given a blood test which exonerated him, but of course the newspapers were full of details of the trial and, from that moment on, anything Chaplin did which did not find favour with the middle-class morality of the kind of people who read *Silver Screen*, *Photoplay* and *Screen Land* was castigated mercilessly by both press and public.

The last film Chaplin made in the United States was *Limelight* (1952), the story of a musical clown who manages to dissuade a dancer (Claire Bloom) from killing herself. There is a moving scene played by Chaplin and Buster Keaton, but otherwise it is only an average film which is really only of interest because Chaplin made it. In 1953, the Chaplin family embarked for England on the *Queen Elizabeth*, and Charlie declared he would never return to the United States. Nor could

Chaplin as a guest of
Churchill at Chartwell at the
age of thirty five.

he, for he was forbidden ever to enter the country after failing to appear
before the House Un-American Activities Committee, led by Senator
Joseph McCarthy (1905-57), which was conducting a farcical witch-
hunt to find Communists amongst members of the cinema industry. It
is not clear why and how Chaplin, or the other unfortunates named by
the Committee, came to be blacklisted. Chaplin may have attracted the
authorities' attention when he made a speech by telephone to 60,000
organized workers who met in Madison Square Park in New York on
22 July 1942. 'People's Artist', 'Comrade' Charlie Chaplin gave a
speech 'in support of President Franklin D. Roosevelt's desire to
immediately open a second front to hasten the eventual defeat of Hitler
and the Axis Powers'.

This speech, containing statements we now know not to have been
totally incorrect, such as 'The fate of the allies is in the hands of the
Communists' appeared in the press all over America. Charlie had
spoken! Earlier, he had made a speech at the request of the American
Committee for Aid to Russia to 10,000 people in San Francisco. After
the Japanese attack on Pearl Harbor the Americans joined the war
against Japan and Germany, but they still left the Russians, who were
being attacked by the Germans, out in the cold. Charlie said in his
speech: 'The Russians are our comrades. They are fighting not only for
their own existence, but for ours as well!' and: 'A Communist mother is
just like any other mother. When she hears the tragic news that her son
will not be coming back, she will weep, just as all mothers weep!'
Russians living in America applauded at length and cried 'Bravo!

Bravo!' But Americans listening to him decided he was a puppet of Moscow, a Communist 'fellow traveler' who, in his naivety, wanted to leave the United States open to the ravages of Bolshevism.

The American public already had something of an ambivalent attitude to their most adored comedian. With *The Great Dictator* (1940), his proper début in the talkies, with Chaplin playing Adenoid Hynkel, the dictator of Tomania (and Jack Oakie playing a brilliant Benzino Napaloni), he sowed the seeds of confusion. This was a parody of Hitler at a time when most Americans knew very little about Hitler other than that he was friendly to America. Chaplin wanted first and foremost to make people laugh in his films, but he put an element of social comment in them as well. He had already shown himself to be a campaigner as well as an entertainer in films like *The Kid* (1920) and *Modern Times* (1936), but this was the first time he delivered a sustained political attack. In Chicago, the cinemas would not show *The Great Dictator*, and the documentary *Inside Nazi Germany* was also banned at the same time. In Tennessee in the early fifties, the cinema industry got together and decided that, owing to Chaplin's political activities and immoral behaviour, they would no longer show his films.

America is an odd country sometimes. Chaplin, who remained British all his life and never became a naturalized American citizen, took his leave of Uncle Sam.

Back in a kind of exile in Britain, and advancing in years, Chaplin made two more films. *A King in New York*, a bitter satire on the McCarthy witch-hunt, was released in 1957. In 1967 he made *A Countess from Hong Kong*, in which Marlon Brando and Sophia Loren played the two leading roles he would normally have reserved for himself and Paulette Goddard, Chaplin directed the film and contented himself with a minor role as an ageing steward.

In 1985, he achieved fame in a new medium: the postage stamp. He appeared on a 29-pence stamp, part of a series which also included Alfred Hitchcock, Peter Sellers, and David Niven.

Charles Chaplin spent the first ten years of his life in severe poverty. All he had to look forward to in life was more of the same misery. But from the age of ten onwards, fortune began to smile on him, and the remainder of his life was a story of wealth and success. Materially and artistically, he was a member of High Society. He died peacefully in his sleep, without having been dogged by illness or infirmity, and he was still alert and creative in his old age. None of his fellow-comedians managed to do this: all the big names of the screen had turbulent lives and died in unhappy circumstances.

This chapter makes no claims to being comprehensive, and it will not catalogue all the people Chaplin worked with in his films. But Edna Purviance (1894-1958) was his leading lady in 35 films, Mabel Normand (1894-1930) in 11, Minta Durfee (1897-1975) in 11 and Cecile Arnold (?) in 7. Phyllis Allen (1861-1938) appeared in 13 Chaplin films, Roscoe Arbuckle (1887-1933) in 6, Billy Armstrong (?) in 11, Albert Austin (1885-1953) in 19, Lloyd Bacon (1890-1955) in 11, Henry Bergman

(1868-1946) in 20, Eric Campbell (1878-1917) in 11, Syd Chaplin (1885-1965) in 5, Charley Chase (1893-1940) in 8, Chester Conklin (1880-1959) in 17, Alice Davenport (b. 1864) in 9, Bud Jamison (1894-1944) in 14, Edgar Kennedy (1890-1948) in 10, Hank Mann (1888-1971) in 9, Harry McCoy (1894-1937) in 11, John Rand (?) in 21, Wesley Ruggles (1889-1972) in 8, Mack Sennett (1880-1960) in 6, Al St John (1893-1963) in 7, Slim Summerville (1892-1946) in 6, Mack Swain (1876-1935) in 17, Ben Turpin (1874-1940) in 4, Leo White (1887-1949) in 21 and Tom Wilson (?) in 6.

Chaplin at a 1972 Royal Gala Charity Performance of *Modern Times* (1936).

Nearly all of Charles Chaplin's films made between 1914 and 1930 are, unfortunately, less funny to a young audience and are becoming increasingly difficult to appreciate. The comedies he made for Keystone, Essanay, Mutual and First National, so highly praised in books on the history of the cinema, are viewed by audiences more used to videos and wide-screen colour feature films as a journey back into the prehistory of film-making. Just as many operas are now not much more than a kind of musical fashion show to many people who were not brought up in that particular culture, so the ageing, flickering black-and-white shorts showing a little man with a moustache and bowler hat pitting his wits against the vicissitudes of fate are little more than mildly amusing melodramas. With a flick of the remote control, we can switch over from Charlie Chaplin's film, *The Rink*, made in 1916, to the umpteenth episode of 'Dallas'.

12
Woody Allen: High-IQ slapstick

Unlike the comedians discussed in previous chapters, Woody Allen is arguably still at the peak of his career, and certainly he is still making films. He is a comedian of our time, not the offspring of vaudeville, music hall or the showboat, but a man who developed his talent for comedy as a gag-writer for newspaper columnists and TV chat-show presenters. He first unleashed his strings of Jewish wisecracks and venomous one-liners, Groucho Marx or Lenny Bruce-style, on audiences in small clubs like The Duplex, The Bitter End and Bonsoir in Greenwich Village. That was in the 1960s, the decade when it was the 'Witz' which determined the trend American comedy took. In the footsteps of comedians Fred Allen, Gracie Allen, Marty Allen and Steve Allen, show business now had a Woody Allen into the bargain.

Woody Allen once told Kathleen Carroll of the New York's *Sunday News* that he thought he was a product of television and the psychiatrist's couch. He told another interviewer that Chaplin's *The Gold Rush* and *City Lights* and Keaton's *The Navigator* and *The General* were four of the greatest films of all time. But whilst it was their physical presence which brought Charlie Chaplin and Buster Keaton their fame, for Woody Allen it is less physical than intellectual acrobatics which he indulges in. He feels much more of a rapport with comedians like Mort Sahl, Groucho Marx, Bob Hope and Syd Caesar than the comedians of Hollywood's golden years.

At least, this is the assumption we shall work on, since Woody Allen has often said contradictory things from one interview to another; he is difficult to get close to and just as difficult to interview.

Because Woody Allen's films, particularly *Play It Again Sam* (1972), *Annie Hall* (1977), *Manhattan* (1979), *Stardust Memories* (1980) and *Hannah and her Sisters* (1986) are full of references to culture and the media, upmarket table-talk, the anxieties of fashionable pseudo-intellectuals having relationship problems and trying hard to crawl out of their 'creative troughs', Woody Allen is a fount of pleasure for cinema journalists, who do not appear to have realized that it is they and their kind whom Allen most often parodies in his films. His world is a convincing one: eavesdrop on any Sloane Square dinner party and you will hear exactly the kind of conversation we hear in Woody Allen's films.

Woody Allen (Allen Stewart Konigsberg, born in 1935, in Flatbush, New York City; he chose 'Woody' as a nickname because of his red hair, which resembles that of Woody Woodpecker), forms no part of the tradition which 'Kings of Comedy' such as Chaplin, Keaton, Lloyd, Langdon and Laurel and Hardy began. Allen makes hardly any use of visual humour, unless we count the comic effect of his own appearance, the prematurely bald Jewish *schlemiel*. His is a kind of high-IQ slapstick, full of high-speed inanity, cynical wisdom, all uttered by a gaunt little man with drooping shoulders. A worried man in his thirties who says to Diane Keaton of his psychiatrist: 'I'm gonna give him one more year, and then I'm goin' to Lourdes!' *(Annie Hall)*

In the same film, Allen says to Shelley Duvall: 'I can't get with any religion that advertises in *Popular Mechanics*.' Diane Keaton wears a tie, a present from 'Grammy' Hall. Says Woody Allen, playing Alvy Singer: 'My granny never gave gifts, you know. She was too busy getting raped by Cossacks.' During Annie and Alvy's not too successful courtship he says he has an erotic technique from Old New Orleans, whereupon he puts a red light-bulb in the lamp and says 'Now we can go about our

Top: Woody Allen. Bottom: *Take the Money and Run* (1969). Allen as the young delinquent Virgil Starkwell being visited in prison by his wife (Janet Margolin).

business here and we can even develop photographs if we want to!'

A non-verbal Woody Allen joke is more often than not over before you even notice it. Annie and Alvy are sitting with a group of friends and Alvy is more or less forced to sniff some coke, ostensibly for his own good, just for the experience. The generous donor of the cocaine says that it cost him $2000. Woody Allen puts the piece of paper bearing the magic white powder to his nose, and promptly sneezes. The coke vanishes like a snowstorm, and immediately we hear a choir singing 'We wish you a Merry Christmas.' This is a long way from the visual gags of Chaplin and Keaton, but somewhat closer to Groucho Marx or W.C.Fields. It is difficult to talk or write about Woody Allen's films without quoting the protagonist. When Annie in *Annie Hall* tells Alvy she likes her college professor and calls him by his Christian name, David, Alvy says: 'David? That's nice – it's a biblical name. And what does he call you? Bathsheba?'

In common with many of the scripts of Bob Hope, Lenny Bruce, Groucho Marx and W.C.Fields, some of Woody Allen's have been published in book form and have become very well-known. 'Not only is there no God, but try getting a plumber on weekends!' or 'Death doesn't make you thirsty, unless you've keeled over after eating a salted herring!' are just two of the one-liners he has to his name. But he is more than simply a creator and deliverer of funny, cynical comments. In *Manhattan,* a black-and-white film with music by George Gershwin and set in what has often been called the cultural centre of the world, the characters have long, drawn-out discussions which require a certain amount of patience and concentration on the part of the viewer. Woody Allen, playing Isaac Davis in the film, says at one point that he has a bitter sense of humour, and this is not so far from the truth. When he and Mary (Diane Keaton) are in bed and she asks him out of the darkness what he is thinking about, the reply is 'I've never had a relationship that's lasted longer than the one between Hitler and Eva Braun!' In *Love and Death* (1975), Boris (Woody Allen) says to his leading lady, Diane Keaton (this time called Sonia), 'What do you mean, God created Man in his own image. Did God ever wear glasses?' Sonia, after a moment's hesitation, replies: 'Well, maybe not with frames like those!'

Although he is a funny man, his purpose is a serious one. His films all have undertones of sadness, with love, death and religion being major themes, not unlike say, Ingmar Bergman. Indeed, by the time he made *Manhattan* Allen was already being hailed as America's Ingmar Bergman. To which he commented: 'Ingrid? At least bisexuality means you have fifty percent more chance of getting a date!'

The intellectual jokes of Woody Allen the entertainer are the result of his talent for sharp observation and an extremely intelligent brain. For many years he visited a psychiatrist almost every day to be treated for a manic-depressive psychosis, and this affected him considerably. He does not smoke, drink or take drugs, and behind the scenes tries to live as sober a life as possible. He does not spend time with his fellow film-makers and does not go to parties held by the Hollywood stars. Every Monday evening he plays the clarinet in The New Orleans Funeral and Ragtime Orchestra, a septet which plays Michael's Pub in the Upper East Side of New York. This was what he was doing on the evening in 1977 when he was awarded three Oscars for *Annie Hall* for best film, best direction and best script (the latter written by Allen and Marshall Brikman). This was the first time since *Citizen Kane* (1941) that the American film industry had honoured an *auteur* who both directed and starred in his own films.

Woody Allen as Leonard Zelig and Mia Farrow as his psychiatrist Dr Eudora Fletcher in *Zelig* (1983).

Woody Allen's father Martin, who did various jobs including being a barkeeper in Sammy's Bowery Follies in Manhattan, and his mother Nettie (a book-keeper in a flower business) gave their son an orthodox Jewish upbringing. He had to attend services on the Sabbath and spent eight years taking Hebrew lessons. The big-city Jewish way of life and Jewish sense of humour have stayed with him, and many studies of his life and work have stated that he is not an actor in the normal sense of the word, but can only play himself, the archetypal neurotic Jew, a somewhat prematurely aged 5ft 3in tall, with the co-ordination and gestures of a schoolboy.

In *The Front*, a serious film which nevertheless has its comic moments, Woody Allen is directed by Martin Ritt and plays Howard Prince, who 'fronts' for TV writer Al Miller, played by Michael Murphy. Miller has been blacklisted by the 'House Un-American Activities Committee' and can no longer publish anything because of his supposed Communist sympathies. So Howard Prince acts as a front for him so that he can still see his scripts being made into television, with all the consequences that entails. The former drugstore cashier eventually ends up sitting in front of the Un-American Activities Committee, and the scene is both dramatic and humorous. Some critics have accused Allen of carrying on with his nightclub routines in front of the camera when the rest of the cast was trying to make a serious film. Director Martin Ritt had himself been blacklisted in the fifties and he certainly had no intention of making a comedy out of his experiences. The film, as it turned out, was a flop in the United States but met with enough success in Europe to make it worthwhile financially.

On the other hand, there are some critics who have attempted to show that Woody Allen's humour is simply a cover for his distinctly bitter message and philosophy: 'After all, life is a concentration camp.' All the searching for hidden symbolism in the work of Woody Allen,

Zelig (1983): Woody Allen, supposedly with Presidents Calvin Coolidge and Herbert Hoover.

the drawing of parallels between his real life and the protagonists of his films (according to the critics, *Annie Hall* was virtually a documentary of Allen's real-life relationship with Diane Keaton): for many people this has spoiled the simple pleasure of watching Woody Allen's films and laughing at them.

It must be said that there is no American TV or film comedian whose work has more to say than that of Woody Allen. When he recounts how he was run over by a car with punctured tyres being pushed by two men, it is almost a joke being made by someone who does not have a particularly high opinion of his fellow men. In some ways he does have a grudge against humanity, or at least the specimens of humanity that appear in his films, such as the narrow-minded expert on McLuhan that stands behind him in the cinema queue in *Annie Hall*. It is in this film that Woody Allen says seriously: 'I feel that life is divided up into the horrible and the miserable.' Anyone (myself included) who has anything to do with the fringes of media society will nod in agreement with this statement. In the advertising business, popular journalism, radio and television or the art world, the Horrible and the Miserable are two categories one constantly bumps into. The paradox is that it is precisely the supposedly cultured up-and-coming young generation of professionals Allen is poking fun at that are also the greatest fans of his

Left: Martin Ritt, director of *The Front* (1976), in which Woody Allen plays a relatively serious role. Right: Allen playing Howard Prince in *The Front*.

films. It is pure pleasure to watch him wreaking havoc amongst these people in his outsize T-shirt.

Woody Allen's films (between 1965 and 1986 he played in nineteen) are ubiquitous in the video hire shops of this world, though in the cinemas it is usually only his most recent film that is shown at any given time. *Zelig* disappeared from the list of films that were big box-office successes in early 1984 and has not reappeared there since. So the pre-recorded video has solved people's problems, especially as Woody Allen's films lend themselves so well to being shown on TV to a couple of people sitting in the lounge at home. Or, as Woody Allen might have added, the bedroom, for it was he who said 'Sex between two people is beautiful; between five people it's fantastic!'

The guardians of America's morality have often accused Woody Allen of being obsessed with sex in all his films. In *Everything You Always Wanted to Know About Sex (But were Afraid to Ask)* (1972) he even appears as a cowardly sperm. In *Zelig*, a masterly comedy documentary about the human chameleon, Leonard Zelig, there is no actual sex as such. Like *Take the Money and Run* (1969) *Zelig* breaks new ground in the genre of fake documentary, complete with a commentator and spurious interviews.

The life story of 'The Incredible Changing Man' is set in the twenties and thirties. Leonard Zelig involuntarily takes on the manner and appearance of people he meets. So he becomes a sportsman when amongst sportsmen, a politician amongst politicians, a rabbi amongst rabbis, and so on. Leonard Zelig is Woody Allen's own *alter ego*: his changes the result of superb use of animation and montage by Gordon Willis, the cameraman, Mel Bourne, the film's designer, editor Susan E. Morse and costume adviser Santo Loquasto. The film makes use of fragments from more than fifty old newsreels from companies like Pathé News, Metrotone, Universal Newsreel and *Wochenschau* from

UFA. Each time, Allen, playing Zelig, actually appears in a genuine
historical scene. So in the Nuremberg Rally of 1933 we see Leonard
dressed in the brown shirt of the SA creeping away behind the Führer in
an attempt to avoid his psychiatrist Dr Eudora Fletcher (Mia Farrow).
He pops up again on the balcony in the Vatican beside Pope Pius XI. It
is impossible to see the joins between the historic scenes and the
fictional ones, especially as Allen plays all his characters with such
bizarre accuracy, and the result is a film that staggered many of its
audiences. If he had used unknown actors to play these parts, the film
might have conned many people into thinking it was a serious
documentary, not least because it has appearances by famous
intellectuals of the 1980s such as Saul Bellow and Susan Sontag adding
their own comments on the person, the agony and the historical role of
Leonard Zelig.

Some publications on Woody Allen recount the story he told years
ago on a TV chat show. Woody Allen was walking along a street in
New York, the city he never leaves for more than a few days. An
'admirer' was tripping along beside him, shouting 'You're a star! Do
you know what you are? A star!!' Muttered Woody Allen: 'What else
am I supposed to be? A Black Hole?'

Woody Woodpecker
© W.L.P., 1946

Postscript

If this book were to be a complete record of all the actors and actresses that starred in American comedies, it would have been a great deal thicker than the one you are holding now. Harry Langdon, Monty Banks, Bobby Vernon, Syd Chaplin, Larry Semon, Billy Bevan, Will Rogers, Ben Turpin, the small fat Joe Cobb from the Our Gang series, Mabel Normand and Roscoe Arbuckle: each of these has their own chapter in the history of silent comedy. And when sound films arrived on the scene, comedians such as the duo of George Arthur and Karl Dane, Joe E. Brown, Eddie Cantor, Danny Kaye, Bob Hope and Bing Crosby, Patsy Kelly and Zasu Pitts, Smith and Dale, Red Skelton, Mickey Rooney, Jimmy Durante and any number of other actors have been excluded from this book. We have selected only the most famous of the screen comedians, and you may have your own favourites.

It is a pity, for example, that Charley Chase, who was active as a comedian as well as a writer and director between 1916 and 1940, hardly ever receives a mention in the annals of comedy nowadays. In 1915 he was working for Mack Sennett; then he moved to Fox Pictures, from 1912 to 1936 he worked at Hal Roach's studios, and from 1937 until his death in 1940 at the age of forty-seven he was making shorts for Columbia. As an actor alone he played in eighty silent two-reelers and sixty sound movies for Hal Roach, and another twenty short comedies for producer Jules White at Columbia. He also appeared in three Hal Roach feature films, of which *Sons of the Desert* (1933, with Laurel and Hardy) and *Kelly the Second* (1936, with Patsy Kelly) were the best.

Charley Chase appeared in burlesque and vaudeville as a teenager. His multitude of talents included tap-dancing and singing, and he played the guitar and other stringed instruments. In his 1936 two-reeler, *The Wrong Trek,* he joins a group of tramps late at night after car

problems, and in this scene he demonstrates once again all his old talents as an entertainer. He joins in a session of barbershop singing and dancing. As he rides along with his fiancée and her mother, they see Laurel and Hardy beside the road, hitch-hiking. Mother-in-law thinks they have 'kind faces', but Charley Chase says 'They look like a couple of horse thieves to me!'

This very brief appearance by Laurel and Hardy is not mentioned at all in the credits, but it was probably a favour to them as friends. A few months after the film was made, Roach sacked Chase following a difference of opinion. Charley Chase wanted to carry on making short comedies, two- and three-reelers or 'featurettes' of fifty minutes or so,

Left: Aged four in 1932, and already a famous film star, George Emmett 'Spanky' McFarland from Hal Roach's 'Our Gang' comedies. Right: Joop P. Smits of Smits Filmdistributie (left) shows the author a 'leader' from a 1916 'Lonesome Luke' film.

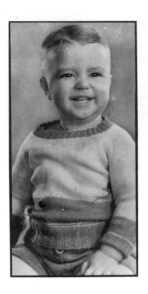

whilst Hal Roach preferred to make feature films for MGM. Charley Chase was a superb joke-writer and was always ready to lend a helping hand to colleagues having trouble on the set by giving them advice or helping them to come up with a good joke. In an interview with *Screen* in May 1940, the man who discovered Laurel and Hardy, Leo McCarey, said of Charley Chase: 'I received credit as a director but it was really Chase who did most of the directing. Whatever success I have had or may have, I owe to his help because he taught me all I know!'

In *Movie Maker* for March 1978 there was an advertisement by an anxious film collector: 'Where have the Charley Chase comedies gone?' Indeed, they are in short supply nowadays. Eight years before, in 1970, the cinema audience could see a few extracts from Charley Chase shorts in a compilation by Robert Youngson called *Four Clowns*. The other three clowns were Stan Laurel, Oliver Hardy and Buster Keaton. This collection of four of the greatest comedians ever is one of the best films of its type, acquainting a public not likely to be familiar with them with the work of Keaton and Chase; this is less the case with Laurel and Hardy, who are far better known.

Despite the boom of the video market, there are still only a few Charley Chase films to be found, and many of these appear on video in tandem with better-known comedians than Charley Chase. The only other alternative is to wait for the rare occasions that they are shown on television.

Generally, though, if you want to see a particular Charley Chase film, or one Chaplin made in 1914, a Harold Lloyd *Lonesome Luke* one-reeler or a 1918 comedy with Stan Laurel playing on his own, you would have a hard time of it. Old films do not have a large market any more, and even a comedy made ten years ago can be hard to track down.

Of course, some collectors and film historians have spent lifetimes building up superb collections of films and stills. These collections may be private, but at least it is reassuring to know that the material is in the hands of people who respect and treasure offerings from the American

Freddie and the Daily Freeloader (CBS television, 1962). Left to right: Mickey Rooney (b.1920), Red Skelton (b.1913) and Jackie Coogan (1914-84), three of America's best-known comedians.

cinema of a bygone age. I have found many impressive film archives amongst these people, a fount of knowledge and a readiness to lend me films and videos. There is not space here to list all those who have helped me in my researches at one time or another, but my thanks go to all of them.

The illustrations are from my own collection of stills, most of them over fifty years old and many rescued from waste-paper baskets. Sometimes they have had to be retouched to conceal sticky tape used to repair them, fold, cuts, comments written on the back and visible on the front, and holes made by drawing-pins, so that they could be printed here. Copyright to them belongs (or used to belong) to Columbia Pictures, Ealing Pictures, Educational Pictures, Hal Roach Studios, First National, Keystone Studios, Metro-Goldwyn-Mayer, Monogram Pictures, Paramount Pictures, RKO Radio Pictures, 20th Century-Fox, United Artists, Universal International, Walter Lantz Productions and Warner Bros.

Are all these comedies really worth all the attention they receive? Perhaps this question is best answered with an anecdote. When a student demonstration in Berlin threatened to become violent, a policeman grabbed the microphone and started telling jokes. That was the end of the demonstration. If you're laughing, you no longer feel like throwing stones at other people.

Filmography

This short filmography gives the title, year of release and name of the studio and/or distributor of each film. More complete filmographies can be found in the books recommended in the Bibliography.

Abbott and Costello

Films featuring Abbott and Costello, made by Universal International unless stated otherwise:

One Night in the Tropics, 1940
Buck Privates, 1941
Hold That Ghost, 1941
In the Navy, 1941
Keep 'Em Flying, 1941
Ride 'Em Cowboy, 1942
Rio Rita, 1942
Pardon My Sarong, 1942
Who Done It?, 1942
It Ain't Hay, 1943
Hit the Ice, 1943
In Society, 1944, Universal
Lost in a Harem, 1944, MGM
The Naughty Nineties, 1945
Abbott and Costello in Hollywood, 1945, MGM
Here Come the Co-Eds, 1945
Little Giant, 1946
The Time of Their Lives, 1946
Buck Privates Come Home, 1947
The Wistful Widow of Wagon Gap, 1947
The Noose Hangs High, 1948, Eagle Lion
Abbott and Costello Meet Frankenstein, 1948
Mexican Hayride, 1948
Abbott and Costello Meet the Killer, Boris Karloff, 1949
Africa Screams, 1949, United Artists
Abbott and Costello in the Foreign Legion, 1950
Abbott and Costello Meet the Invisible Man, 1951
Comin' Round the Mountain, 1951
Jack and the Beanstalk, 1952, Warner

Lost in Alaska, 1952
Abbott and Costello Meet Captain Kydd, 1953, Warner
Abbott and Costello Go to Mars, 1953
Abbott and Costello Meet Dr Jekyll and Mr Hyde, 1953
Abbott and Costello Meet the Keystone Cops, 1955
Abbott and Costello Meet the Mummy, 1955
Dance With Me, Henry, 1956, UA
The World of Abbott and Costello, 1965 (compilation)
The Abbott and Costello Show, 1952/1954, CBS, 52 episodes

Lou Costello made a guest appearance in:

The 30-Foot Bridge of Candy Rock, 1959, Columbia

Harold Lloyd

The films of Harold Lloyd *(shorts)*, distributed by Pathé:

1915
Just Nuts
Lonesome Luke
A Mixup for Masie
Some Baby
Giving Them Fits
Bughouse Bellhops
Great While It Lasted
Ragtime Snap Shots
A Fozzle at the Tea Party
Ruses, Rhymes and Roughnecks
Peculiar Patients' Pranks
Lonesome Luke, Social Gangster

1916
Lonesome Luke Leans to the Literary
Luke Lugs Luggage
Lonesome Luke Lolls in Luxury
Luke, the Candy Cut-Up
Luke Foils the Villain
Luke and the Rural Roughnecks
Luke Pipes the Pippens
Lonesome Luke, Circus King
Luke's Double
Them Was the Happy Days
Luke and the Bomb Throwers
Luke's Late Lunchers
Luke Laughs Last
Luke's Fatal Flivver
Luke's Society Mixup
Luke's Washful Waiting
Luke Rides Rough-Shod
Luke, Crystal Gazer
Luke's Lost Lamb
Luke Does the Midway
Luke joins the Navy
Luke and the Mermaids
Luke's Speedy Club Life
Luke and the Bangtails
Luke the Chauffeur
Luke's Preparedness Preparations
Luke the Gladiator
Luke, Patient Provider
Luke's Newsie Knockout
Luke's Movie Muddle
Luke, Rank Impersonator
Luke's Fireworks Fizzle
Luke Locates the Loot
Luke's Shattered Sleep

1917
Luke's Lost Liberty

Luke's Busy Day
Luke's Trolley Troubles
Lonesome Luke, Lawyer
Luke Wins Ye Ladye Fair
Lonesome Luke's Lively Life
Lonesome Luke on Tin Can Alley
Lonesome Luke's Honeymoon
Lonesome Luke, Plumber
Stop! Luke! Listen!
Lonesome Luke, Messenger
Lonesome Luke, Mechanic
Lonesome Luke's Wild Women
Over the Fence
Lonesome Luke Loses Patients
Pinched
By the Sad Sea Waves
Birds of a Feather
Bliss
Lonesome Luke in From London to Laramie
Rainbow Island
Lonesome Luke in Love, Laughs and Lather
The Flirt
Clubs are Trump
All Aboard
We Never Sleep
Move On
Bashful

1918
The Tip
The Big Idea

The Lamb
Hit Him Again
Beat It
A Gasoline Wedding
Look Pleasant, Please
Here Come the Girls
Let's Go
On the Jump
Follow the Crowd
Pipe the Whiskers
It's a Wild Life
Hey There
Kicked Out
The Non-Stop Kid
Two-Gun Gussie
Fireman, Save My Child
The City Slicker
Sic 'Em Towser
Somewhere in Turkey
Are Crooks Dishonest?
An Ozark Romance
Kicking the Germ Out of Germany
That's Him
Bride and Gloom
Two Scrambled
Bees in His Bonnet
Swing Your Partners
Why Pick on Me?
Nothing but Trouble
Hear 'Em Rave
Take a Chance
She Loves Me Not

1919
Wanted — $5,000
Going! Going! Gone
As Father
On the Fire
I'm On My Way
Look Out Below!
The Dutiful Dub

Next Aisle Over
A Sammy in Siberia
Just Dropped In
Crack Your Heels
Ring Up the Curtain
Young Mr Jazz
Si Senor
Before Breakfast
The Marathon
Back to the Woods
Pistols for Breakfast
Swat the Crook
Off the Trolley
Spring Fever
Billy Blazes, Esq.
Just Neighbors
At the Old Stage Door
Never Touched me
A Jazzed Honeymoon
Count Your Change
Chop Suey & Co.
Heap Big Chief
Don't Shove
Be My Wife
The Rajah
He Leads, Others Follow
Soft Money
Count the Votes
Pay Your Dues
His Only Father
Bumping into Broadway
Captain Kidd's Kids
From Hand to Mouth

1920
His Royal Slyness
Haunted Spooks
An Eastern Westerner
High and Dizzy
Get Out and Get Under
Number Please

1921
Now or Never
Among Those Present
I Do
Never Weaken

The feature films of Harold Lloyd:

A Sailor-Made Man, 1921, Associated Exhibitors
Grandma's Boy, 1922, Associated Exhibitors
Dr Jack, 1923, Pathé
Safety Last, 1923, Pathé
Why Worry?, 1923, Pathé
Girl Shy, 1924, Pathé
Hot Water, 1924, Pathé
The Freshman, 1925, Pathé
For Heaven's Sake, 1926, Paramount

The Kidd Brother, 1927, Paramount
Speedy, 1928, Paramount
Welcome Danger, 1929, Paramount
Feet First, 1930, Paramount
Movie Crazy, 1932, Paramount
The Cat's-Paw, 1934, Fox
The Milky Way, 1936, Paramount
Professor Beware, 1938, Paramount
The Sin of Harold Diddlebock, 1947, UA*

*Also distributed as *Mad Wednesday*.
Compilations:

Harold Lloyd's World of Comedy, 1962, Continental
Distributors
The Funny Side of Life, 1963, Harold Lloyd Productions

The Marx Brothers

The films of the Marx Brothers:

The Cocoanuts, 1929, Paramount
Animal Crackers, 1930, Paramount
Monkey Business, 1931, Paramount
Horse Feathers, 1932, Paramount
Duck Soup, 1933, Paramount
A Night at the Opera, 1935, MGM
A Day at the Races, 1937, MGM
Room Service, 1938, RKO
At the Circus, 1939, MGM
Go West, 1940, MGM
The Big Store, 1941, MGM
A Night in Casablanca, 1946, UA
Love Happy, 1949, UA

Screen Snapshots No. 2, 1943, Columbia
Screen Snapshots No. 3, 1943, Columbia
Stage Door Canteen, 1943, UA
All-Star Bond Rally, 1945, Fox
Copacabana, 1947, UA
Mr Music, 1950, Paramount
Double Dynamite, 1951, RKO
A Girl in Every Port, 1952, RKO
Will Success Spoil Rock Hunter?, 1957, Fox
The Story of Mankind, 1957, Warner
Showdown at Alcer Gulch, 1958, Saturday Evening
Post Production
Skidoo, 1968, Paramount

In 1926 the Marx Brothers made their own film,
which was never distributed:

Humorisk

The Marx Brothers also appeared together or
separately in the following:

Too Many Kisses, 1925, Paramount
Hollywood on Parade, 1932, Paramount
Hollywood on Parade, 1933, Paramount
La Fiesta de Santa Barbara, 1935, MGM
The King and the Chorus Girl, 1937, Warner

Television work of Groucho Marx

You Bet Your Life, 1950 & 62, NBC (renamed The Groucho
Show — 1962)
You Bet Your Life *reruns* shown as: The Best of Groucho

George Formby

George Formby made his début as a child in 1914 in a film by the English film pioneer, Will Barker:

By the Shortest of Heads

Twenty years later he made his first feature:

Boots Boots, 1934

The films of George Formby made at Ealing Studios:

No Limit, 1935
Keep Your Seats Please, 1936
Feather Your Nest, 1937
Keep Fit, 1937
I See Ice, 1938
It's in the Air, 1938
Trouble Brewing, 1939
Come On George, 1939
Let George Do It, 1940
Spare a Copper, 1940
Turned Out Nice Again, 1941

The films of George Formby distributed by Columbia-British:

South American George, 1942
She Snoops to Conquer, 1944
I Didn't Do It, 1945
Remember the Unicorn, 1946
Bell Bottom George, 1946
George in Civvy Street, 1946

Laurel and Hardy

The films of Laurel and Hardy (*shorts*) made at Hal Roach Studios:

Forty-Five Minutes from Hollywood, 1926
Duck Soup, 1927
Slipping Wives, 1927
Love 'Em and Weep, 1927
Why Girls Love Sailors, 1927
With Love and Hisses, 1927

Sailors Beware!, 1927
Do Detectives Think?, 1927
Flying Elephants, 1927
Sugar Daddies, 1927
The Call of the Cuckoo, 1927
The Second Hundred Years, 1927
Hatts Off, 1927
Putting Pants on Philip, 1927
The Battle of the Century, 1927
Leave 'Em Laughing, 1928
The Finishing Touch, 1928
From Soup to Nuts, 1928
You're Darn Tootin', 1928
Their Purple Moment, 1928
Should Married Men Go Home?, 1928
Early to Bed, 1928
Two Tars, 1928
Habeas Corpus, 1928

We Faw Down, 1928
Liberty, 1928
Wrong Again, 1929
That's My Wife, 1929
Big Business, 1929
Double Whoopee, 1929
Unaccustomed As We Are, 1929
Berth Marks, 1929
Men O'War, 1929
Perfect Day, 1929
They Go Boom, 1929
Bacon Grabbers, 1929
The Hoose-gow, 1929
Angora Love, 1929
Night Owls, 1930
Blotto, 1930
Brats, 1930
Below Zero, 1930
Hog Wild, 1930
The Laurel & Hardy Murder Case, 1930
Another Fine Mess, 1930
Be Big, 1930
Chickens Come Home, 1931
Laughing Gravy, 1931
Our Wife, 1931
Come Clean, 1931
One Good Turn, 1931
Helpmates, 1931
Any Old Port, 1932
The Music Box, 1932
The Chimp, 1932
County Hospital, 1932
Scram!, 1932
Their First Mistake, 1932
Towed in a Hole, 1933
Twice Two, 1933
Me and My Pal, 1933
The Midnight Patrol, 1933
Busy Bodies, 1933
Dirty Work, 1933
Oliver the Eighth, 1934
Going Bye-Bye, 1934
Them Thar Hills, 1934
The Live Ghost, 1934
Tit for Tat, 1935
The Fixer Uppers, 1935
Thicker Than Water, 1935

Laurel and Hardy's feature films:

Pardon Us, 1931, Roach
Pack Up Your Troubles, 1932, Roach
Fra Diavolo, 1933, Roach
Sons of the Desert, 1933, Roach
Babes in Toyland, 1934, Roach
Bonnie Scotland, 1935, Roach
The Bohemian Girl, 1936, Roach
Our Relations, 1936
Way Out West, 1937, Roach
Swiss Miss, 1938, Roach
Blockheads, 1938, Roach
Flying Deuces, 1939, Boris Morros/RKO
A Chump at Oxford, 1940, Roach

Saps at Sea, 1940, Roach
Great Guns, 1941, Fox
A Haunting We Will Go, 1942, Fox
Air Raid Wardens, 1943, MGM
Jitterbugs, 1943, Fox
Dancing Masters, 1943, Fox
The Big Noise, 1944, Fox
The Bullfighters, 1945, Fox
Nothing But Trouble, 1945, MGM
Atoll K, 1951, Sirius/Fortezza

Laurel and Hardy made guest appearances in:

The Hollywood Revue of 1929, 1929, MGM
The Slippery Pearls, 1932, RKO
Wild Poses, 1933, Roach
On the Wrong Trek, 1936, Roach
Tree in a Test Tube, 1943, US Government

Compilations:

The Golden Age of Comedy, 1958, DCA
When Comedy Was King, 1960, 20th Century-Fox
Days of Thrills and Laughter, 1961, 20th Century-Fox
Thirty Years of Fun, 1962, 20th Century-Fox
MGM's Big Parade of Laughs, 1964, MGM
Laurel and Hardy's Laughing Twenties, 1965, MGM
The Crazy World of Laurel and Hardy, 1966, Jay
Ward Productions
The Further Perils of Laurel and Hardy, 1967, RYP
Four Clowns, 1970, 20th Century-Fox

W.C. Fields

The films of W.C. Fields (*shorts*):

Pool Sharks, 1915, Gaumont
The Golf Specialist, 1930, RKO
The Dentist, 1932, Sennett/Paramount
The Fatal Glass of Beer, 1933, Sennett/Paramount
The Pharmacist, 1933, Sennett/Paramount
The Barber Shop, 1933, Sennett/Paramount

The feature films of W.C. Fields:

Janice Meredith, 1924, Metro/Goldwyn
Sally of the Sawdust, 1925, UA
That Royle Girl, 1926, Paramount
It's the Old Army Game, 1926, Paramount
So's Your Old Man, 1926, Paramount
The Potters, 1927, Paramount
Running Wild, 1927, Paramount
Two Flaming Youths, 1927, Paramount
Tillie's Punctured Romance, 1928, Paramount
Fools for Luck, 1928, Paramount
Her Majesty, Love, 1931, First National
Million Dollar Legs, 1932, Paramount
If I Had a Million, 1932, Paramount
International House, 1933, Paramount
Tillie and Gus, 1933, Paramount
Alice in Wonderland, 1933, Paramount
Six of a Kind, 1934, Paramount
You're Telling Me, 1934, Paramount
The Old-Fashioned Way, 1934, Paramount
Mrs. Wiggs's Cabbage Patch, 1934, Paramount

It's A Gift, 1934, Paramount
David Copperfield, 1935, MGM
Mississippi, 1935, Paramount
The Man on the Flying Trapeze, 1935, Paramount
Poppy, 1936, Paramount
The Big Broadcast of 1938, 1938, Paramount
You Can't Cheat an Honest Man, 1939, Universal
My Little Chickadee, 1940, Universal
The Bank Dick, 1940, Universal
Never Give a Sucker an Even Break, 1941, Universal
Follow the Boys, 1944, Universal
Song of the Open Road, 1944, UA
Sensations of 1945, 1944, UA

Rod Steiger played W.C. Fields in a Universal film based on the book by Carlotta Monti, *W.C. Fields and Me* (1979)

Lucille Ball

The films of Lucille Ball:

Broadway Thru a Keyhole, 1933, United Artists
Blood Money, 1933, United Artists
Roman Scandals, 1933, United Artists
Moulin Rouge, 1934, United Artists
Nana, 1934, United Artists
Bottoms Up, 1934, Fox
Hold That Girl, 1934, Fox
Bulldog Drummond Strikes Back, 1934, United Artists

The Affairs of Cellini, 1934, UA
Kid Millions, 1934, UA
Broadway Bill, 1934, Columbia
Jealousy, 1934, Columbia
Men of the Night, 1934, Columbia
The Fugitive Lady, 1934, Columbia
Carnival, 1935, Columbia
The Whole Town's Talking, 1935, Columbia
Roberta, 1935, RKO
Old Man Rhythm, 1935, RKO
The Three Musketeers, 1935, RKO
Top Hat, 1935, RKO
I Dream Too Much, 1935, RKO
Chatterbox, 1936, RKO
The Farmer in the Dell, 1936, RKO
Follow the Fleet, 1936, RKO
Bunker Bean, 1936, RKO
That Girl from Paris, 1936, RKO
Winterset, 1936, RKO

Don't Tell the Wife, 1937, RKO
Stage Door, 1937, RKO
Joy of Living, 1938, RKO
Go Chase Yourself, 1938, RKO
Having Wonderful Time, 1938, RKO
The Affairs of Annabel, 1938, RKO
Room Service, 1938, RKO
The Next Time I Marry, 1938, RKO
Annabel Takes a Tour, 1938, RKO
Beauty for the Asking, 1939, RKO
Twelve Crowded Hours, 1939, RKO
Panama Lady, 1939, RKO
Five Came Back, 1939, RKO
That's Right, You're Wrong, 1939, RKO
The Marines Fly High, 1940, RKO
You Can't Fool Your Wife, 1940, RKO
Dance, Girl, Dance, 1940, RKO
Too Many Girls, 1940, RKO
A Girl, a Guy and a Gob, 1941, RKO
Look Who's Laughing, 1941, RKO
Valley of the Sun, 1942, RKO
The Big Street, 1942, RKO
Seven Day's Leave, 1942, RKO
DuBarry Was a Lady, 1943, MGM
Best Foot Forward, 1943, MGM
Thousands Cheer, 1943, MGM
Meet the People, 1944, MGM
Without Love, 1945, MGM

Abbott and Costello in Hollywood, 1945, MGM
Ziegfeld Follies, 1946, MGM
The Dark Corner, 1946, Fox
Easy to Wed, 1946, MGM
Two Smart People, 1946, MGM
Lover Come Back, 1946, Universal
Lured, 1947, UA
Her Husband's Affairs, 1947, Columbia
Sorrowful Jones, 1949, Paramount
Easy Living, 1949, RKO
Miss Grant Takes Richmond, 1949, Columbia
Fancy Pants, 1950, Paramount
The Fuller Brush Girl, 1950, Columbia
The Magic Carpet, 1951, Columbia
The Long, Long Trailer, 1954, MGM
Forever, Darling, 1956, MGM
The Facts of Life, 1960, UA
Critic's Choice, 1963, Warner
A Guide for the Married Man, 1967, Fox
Yours, Mine and Ours, 1968, UA
Mame, 1974, Warner

Television series of Lucille Ball:

I Love Lucy, 1951-57, CBS, 179 episodes
The Lucy Show, 1961-68, CBS, 156 episodes
Here's Lucy, 1968-74, CBS, 144 episodes

The Three Stooges

The films of The Three Stooges (*shorts*) with Ted Healy, made by MGM:

Nertsery Rhymes, 1933
Beer and Pretzels, 1933

Hello Pop, 1933
Plane Nuts, 1933
The Big Idea, 1934

Two-reelers (less than twenty minutes) made by Columbia Pictures:

Woman Haters, 1934
Punch Drunks, 1934
Men in Black, 1934
Three Little Pigskins, 1934

Horse Collars, 1935
Restless Knights, 1935
Pop Goes the Easel, 1935
Uncivil Warriors, 1935
Pardon My Scots, 1935
Hoi Polloi, 1935
Three Little Beers, 1935
Ants in the Pantry, 1936
Movie Maniacs, 1936
Half-Shot Shooters, 1936
Disorder in the Court, 1936
A Pain in the Pullman, 1936
False Alarms, 1936
Whoop I'm an Indian, 1936
Slippery Silks, 1936
Grips, Grunts and Groans, 1937
Dizzy Doctors, 1937
Three Dumb Clucks, 1937
Back to the Woods, 1937
Goofs and Saddles, 1937
Cash and Carry, 1937
Playing the Ponies, 1937
The Sitter-Downers, 1937
Termites of 1938, 1938
Wee Wee Monsieur, 1938
Tassels in the Air, 1938
Flat Foot Stooges, 1938
Healthy, Wealthy and Dumb, 1938
Violent is the Word for Curly, 1938
Three Missing Links, 1938
Mutts to You, 1938
Three Little Sew and Sews, 1939
We Want Our Mummy, 1939
A-Ducking They Did Go, 1939
Yes, We Have No Bonanza, 1939
Saved by the Belle, 1939
Calling All Curs, 1939
Oily to Bed, Oily to Rise, 1939
Three Sappy People, 1939
You Nazity Spy, 1940
Rockin' Through the Rockies, 1940
A-Plumbing We Will Go, 1940
Nutty But Nice, 1940
How High Is Up?, 1940
From Nurse to Worse, 1940
No Census, No Feeling, 1940
Cookoo Cavaliers, 1940
Boobs in Arms, 1940
So Long, Mr Chumps, 1941
Dutiful but Dumb, 1941
All the World's a Stooges, 1941
I'll Never Heil Again, 1941
An Ache in Every Stake, 1941
In the Sweet Pie and Pie, 1941
Some More of Samoa, 1941
Loco Boy Makes Good, 1942
Cactus Makes Perfect, 1942
What's the Matador?, 1942
Matri-Phony, 1942
Three Smart Saps, 1942
Even as I.O.U., 1942
Sock-a-Bye Baby, 1942
They Stooge to Conga, 1942
Dizzy Detectives, 1943
Spook Louder, 1943

Back from the Front, 1943
Three Little Twirps, 1943
Higher Than a Kite, 1943
I Can Hardly Wait, 1943
Dizzy Pilots, 1943
Phony Express, 1943
A Gem of a Jam, 1943
Crash Goes the Hash, 1944
Busy Buddies, 1944
The Yoke's on Me, 1944
Idle Roomers, 1944
Gents Without Cents, 1945
No Dough, Boys, 1945
Three Pests in a Mess, 1945
Boody Dupes, 1945
If a Body Meets a Body, 1945
Micro-Phonies, 1945
Beer Barrel Polecats, 1946
A Bird in the Hand, 1946
Uncivil Warbirds, 1946
The Three Troubledoers, 1946
Monkey Businessmen, 1946
Three Loan Wolves, 1946
G.I. Wanna Home, 1946
Rhythm and Weep, 1946
Three Little Pirates, 1946
Half-Wits Holiday, 1947
Fright Night, 1947
Out West, 1947
Hold That Lion, 1947
Brideless Groom, 1947
Sing a Song of Six Pants, 1947
All Gummed Up, 1947
Shivering Sherlocks, 1948

Pardon My Clutch, 1948
Squareheads of the Round Table, 1948
Fiddlers Three, 1948
Heavenly Daze, 1948
Hot Scots, 1948
I'm a Monkey's Uncle, 1948
Mummy's Dummies, 1948
Crime on Their Hands, 1948
The Ghost Talks, 1949
Who Done It?, 1949
Hokus Pokus, 1949
Fuelin' Around, 1949
Malice in the Palace, 1949
Vagabond Loafers, 1949
Dunked in the Deep, 1949
Punchy Cowpunchers, 1950
Hugs and Mugs, 1950
Dopey Dicks, 1950
Love at First Bite, 1950
Self Made Maids, 1950
Three Hams on Rye, 1950
Studio Stoops, 1950
Slaphappy Sleuths, 1950
A Snitch in Time, 1950
Three Arabian Nuts, 1950
Baby Sitters' Jitters, 1951
Don't Throw That Knife, 1951
Scrambled Brains, 1951
Merry Mavericks, 1951
The Tooth Will Out, 1951
Hula-La-La, 1951
Pest Man Wins, 1951
A Missed Fortune, 1952
Listen, Judge, 1952
Corny Casanovas, 1952
He Cooked His Goose, 1952
Gents in a Jam, 1952
Three Dark Horses, 1952
Cookoo on a Choochoo, 1952
Up in Daisy's Penthouse, 1953
Booty and the Beat, 1953
Loose Loot, 1953
Tricky Dicks, 1953
Spooks, 1953
Pardon My Backfire, 1953
Rip, Sew and Stitch, 1953
Bubble Trouble, 1953
Goof on the Roof, 1953
Income Tax Sappy, 1954
Musty Musketeers, 1954
Pals and Gals, 1954
Knutzy Knights, 1954
Shot in the Frontier, 1954
Scotched in Scotland, 1954
Fling in the Ring, 1955
Of Cash and Hash, 1955
Gypped in the Penthouse, 1955
Bedlam in Paradise, 1955
Stone Age Romeos, 1955
Wham-Bam-Slam, 1955
Hot Ice, 1955
Blunder Boys, 1955
Husband Beware, 1956
Creeps, 1956
Flagpole Jitters, 1956

For Crimin' Out Loud, 1956
Rumpus in the Harem, 1956
Hot Stuff, 1956
Scheming Schemers, 1956
Commotion on the Ocean, 1956
Hoofs and Goofs, 1957
Muscle Up a Little Closer, 1957
A Merry Mix Up, 1957
Space Ship Sappy, 1957
Guns a Poppin', 1957
Horsing Around, 1957
Rusty Romeos, 1957
Outer Space Jitters, 1957
Quiz Whiz, 1958
Fifi Blows Her Top, 1958
Pies and Guys, 1958
Sweet and Hot, 1958
Flying Saucer Daffy, 1958
Oil's Well That Ends Well, 1958
Triple Crossed, 1959
Sappy Bullfighters, 1959

Feature films distributed by Columbia:

Rockin' in the Rockies, 1945
Have Rocket, Will Travel, 1959
The Three Stooges Meet Hercules, 1962
The Three Stooges in Orbit, 1962
The Three Stooges Go Around the World in a Daze, 1963
The Outlaws IS Coming, 1965

Feature films in which The Three Stooges made guest appearances:

Soup to Nuts, 1930, Fox
Turn Back the Clock, 1933, MGM
Meet the Baron, 1933, MGM
Dancing Lady, 1933, MGM
Fugitive Lovers, 1934, MGM
Hollywood Party, 1934, MGM
The Captain Hates the Sea, 1934, Columbia
Start Cheering, 1938, Columbia
Time Out for Rhythm, 1941
My Sister Eileen, 1942
Swing Parade of 1946, 1946, Monogram
Gold Raiders, 1951, United Artists
Snow White and the Three Stooges, 1961, Fox
It's a Mad Mad Mad Mad World, 1963, UA
Four for Texas, 1963, Warner

The Three Stooges made 190 two-reelers for Columbia Pictures, 97 with Curly Howard, 77 with Shemp Howard and 16 with Joe Besser.

Dean Martin and Jerry Lewis

The films of Dean Martin and Jerry Lewis made by
Paramount Pictures (the addition of York
Productions to the title credits refers to a paper
company set up by Martin and Lewis. The films
were produced and distributed by Paramount).

My Friend Irma, 1949
My Friend Irma Goes West, 1950
At War With the Army, 1950
That's My Boy, 1951
Sailor Beware, 1951
Jumping Jacks, 1952
The Stooge, 1953
Scared Stiff, 1953
The Caddy, 1953
Money from Home, 1953
Living It Up, 1954
Three Ring Circus, 1954
You're Never Too Young, 1955
Artists and Models, 1955
Pardners, 1956
Hollywood or Bust, 1956

Martin and Lewis made a guest appearance in:

Road to Bali, 1952, Paramount

Solo films of Jerry Lewis:

The Delicate Delinquent, 1957, Paramount
The Sad Sack, 1958, Paramount
Rock-a-Bye-Baby, 1958, Paramount
The Geisha Boy, 1958, Paramount
Don't Give Up the Ship, 1959, Paramount
Visit to a Small Planet, 1960, Paramount
The Bellboy, 1960, Paramount
Cinderfella, 1960, Paramount
The Ladies' Man, 1961, Paramount
The Errand Boy, 1961, Paramount
It's Only Money, 1962, Paramount
The Nutty Professor, 1963, Paramount
Who's Minding the Store, 1964, Paramount
The Patsy, 1964, Paramount
The Disorderly Orderly, 1964, Paramount
The Family Jewels, 1965, Paramount
Boeing-Boeing, 1965, Paramount
Three on a Couch, 1966, Columbia
Way, Way Out! 1966, 20th Century-Fox
The Big Mouth, 1967, Columbia

Don't Raise the Bridge, Lower the River, 1968, Columbia
Hook, Line and Sinker, 1969, Columbia
Which Way to the Front?, 1970, Warner
Hardly Working, 1979, Gold Coast
The King of Comedy, 1983, EI/Fox

Jerry Lewis made a guest appearance in:

Li'l Abner, 1959, Paramount
It's a Mad Mad Mad Mad World, 1963, UA

Television work of Jerry Lewis:

The Jerry Lewis Show, 1963, ABC
The Jerry Lewis Show, 1967-69, NBC
The Jerry Lewis Labor Day Telethon

Buster Keaton

The films of Buster Keaton *(shorts)* distributed by Paramount Famous Players-Lasky:

The Butcher Boy, 1917
A Reckless Romeo, 1917
Rough House, 1917
His Wedding Night, 1917
Oh, Doctor, 1917
Fatty at Coney Island, 1917
A Country Hero, 1917
Out West, 1918
The Bell Boy, 1918
Moonshine, 1918
Good Night, Nurse!, 1918
The Cook, 1918
A Desert Hero, 1919
Back Stage, 1919
The Hayseed, 1919
The Garage, 1919

The films of Buster Keaton *(shorts)* distributed by Metro Pictures Corporation:

The High Sign, 1920
One Week, 1920
Convict 13, 1920
The Scare Crow, 1920
Neighbors, 1920
The Haunted House, 1921
Hard Luck, 1921
The Goat, 1921

The films of Buster Keaton *(shorts)* distributed by First National:

The Playhouse, 1921
The Boat, 1921
The Paleface, 1921
Cops, 1922
My Wife's Relations, 1922
The Blacksmith, 1922
The Frozen North, 1922
Day Dreams, 1922
The Electric House, 1922
The Balloonatic, 1923
The Love Nest, 1923

The feature films of Buster Keaton:

The Saphead, 1920, Metro

Three Ages, 1923, Metro
Our Hospitality, 1923, Metro
Sherlock Jr., 1924, Metro
The Navigator, 1924, Metro/Goldwyn
Seven Chances, 1925, Metro/Goldwyn
Go West, 1925, Metro/Goldwyn
Battling Butler, 1926, Metro/Goldwyn
The General, 1927, Metro/Goldwyn
College, 1927, UA
Steamboat Bill Jr., 1928, UA
The Cameraman, 1928, MGM
Spite Marriage, 1929, MGM
Free and Easy, 1930, MGM
Doughboys, 1930, MGM
Parlor, Bedroom and Bath, 1931, MGM
Sidewalks of New York, 1931, MGM
The Passionate Plumber, 1932, MGM
Speak Easily, 1932, MGM
What! No Beer?, 1933, MGM
Le Roi des Champs-Elysées, 1934, France
The Invader, 1936, MGM-British
The Villain Still Pursued Her, 1940, RKO
Li'l Abner, 1940, RKO
Tales of Manhattan, 1942, Fox
Forever and a Day, 1943, RKO
San Diego, I Love You, 1944, Universal
That's the Spirit, 1945, Universal
The Night With You, 1945, Universal
El Moderno Barba Azul, 1946, Mexico
God's Country, 1946, Screen Guild
In the Good Old Summertime, 1949, MGM
You're My Everything, 1949, Fox
Sunset Boulevard, 1950, Paramount
Limelight, 1952, UA
L'Incantevole Nemica, 1952, Italy
Around the World in 80 Days, 1956, UA
The Adventures of Huckleberry Finn, 1960, MGM
Pajama Party, 1964, AI

Beach Blanket Bingo, 1965, AI
Due Marinese e Uno Generale, 1965, Italy
How to Stuff a Wild Bikini, 1965, AI
Sergeant Deadhead, AI
A Funny Thing Happened on the Way to the Forum,
1966, UA

Television work of Buster Keaton:

Life With Buster Keaton, 1952 (compilation)
The Buster Keaton Show, 1957, KTTV, Hollywood

Charles Chaplin

The films of Charles Chaplin made by Mack Sennett
at Keystone Studios in 1914:

Making a Living
Kid Auto Races at Venice
Mabel's Strange Predicament
Between Showers
A Film Johnny
Tango Tangles
His Favourite Pastime
Cruel, Cruel Love
The Star Boarder
Mabel at the Wheel
Twenty Minutes of Love
Caught in a Cabaret
Caught in the Rain
A Busy Day
The Fatal Mallet
Her Friend the Bandit
The Knockout
Mabel's Busy Day
Mabel's Married Life
Laughing Gas
The Property Man
The Face on the Bar Room Floor
Recreation
The Masquerader
His New Profession
The Rounders
The New Janitor
Those Love Pangs
Dough and Dynamite
Gentlemen of Nerve
His Musical Career
His Trysting Place
Tillie's Punctured Romance*
Getting Acquainted
His Prehistoric Past

*Until this film, all Chaplin's films had been
'split-reel' (about four minutes), single-
reel (eight or nine minutes) or two reels
(approximately eighteen minutes). *Tillie's
Punctured Romance* was six reels long and
thus the first long comedy film ever.
Depending on how fast the projectionist
showed the film (16-18 frames per second)
the film would last about an hour.

Films of Charles Chaplin made in 1915 at Essanay
Studios:

His New Job
A Night Out
The Champion
In the Park
The Jitney Elopement
The Tramp
By the Sea
Work
A Woman
The Bank
Shanghaied
A Night at the Show
Carmen
Police
Triple Trouble

Films of Charles Chaplin made in 1916/17 at
Mutual Studios:

The Floorwalker
The Fireman
The Vagabond
One A.M.
The Count
The Pawnshop
Behind the Screen
The Rink
Easy Street
The Cure
The Immigrant
The Adventurer

Films of Charles Chaplin made in his own studio
and distributed by First National:

A Dog's Life, 1918
The Bond, 1918
Shoulder Arms, 1918
Sunnyside, 1919
A Day's Pleasure, 1919
The Kid, 1921
The Idle Class, 1920
Pay Day, 1922
The Pilgrim, 1923

Features of Charles Chaplin distributed by United
Artists:

A Woman of Paris, 1923

The Gold Rush, 1925
The Circus, 1928
City Lights, 1931
Modern Times, 1936
The Great Dictator, 1940
Monsieur Verdoux, 1947
Limelight, 1952
A King in New York, 1957
A Countess from Hong Kong, 1966

Compilations of extracts from Chaplin's shorts and features:

Chaplin Festival, 1943
That's Charley!, 1952
The Chaplin Revue, 1959
Merry Go Round, 1962
Chaplin's Art of Comedy, 1969

Films by Charles Chaplin that have been brought out under various titles at different times:

Making a Living, 1914
   A Busted Johnny
   Troubles
Kid Auto Races at Venice, 1914
   The Children's Automobile Race
Mabel's Strange Predicament, 1914
   Hotel Mixup
Between Showers, 1914
   Charlie and the Umbrella
   In Wrong
A Film Johnny, 1914
   Charlie at the Studio
   Movie Nut
Tango, Tangles, 1914
   Music Hall
His Favourite Pastime, 1914
   Reckless Fling
   The Bonehead
Cruel, Cruel Love, 1914
   Lord Help Us
The Star Boarder, 1914
   Landlady's Pet
   In Love with his Landlady
Mabel at the Wheel, 1914
   Hot Finish
   His Daredevil Queen
Twenty Minutes of Love, 1914
   Cops and Watches
   Love-Fried
Caught in a Cabaret, 1914
   Faking with Society
   Jazz Waiter
Caught in the Rain, 1914
   At it Again
   In the Park
   Who Got Stung?
A Busy Day, 1914
   Lady Charlie

The Fatal Mallet, 1914
   The Rival Suitors
   The Pile Driver
   Hit Him Again
Her Friend the Bandit, 1914
   Mabel's Flirtation
   A Thief Catcher
The Knockout, 1914
   The Pugilist
   Counted Out
Mabel's Busy Day, 1914
   Love and Lunch
   Hot Dogs
   Charlie and the Sausages
Mabel's Married Life, 1914
   The Squarehead
   When You're Married
Laughing Gas, 1914
   The Dentist
   Down and Out
   Tuning his Ivories
   Bust Little Dentist
The Property Man, 1914
   The Rustabout
   Vamping Venus
The Face on the Bar Room Floor, 1914
   The Ham Actor
   The Ham Artist
Recreation, 1914
   Spring Fever
The Masquerader, 1914
   The Female Impersonator
   His New Profession
   Putting One Over
His New Profession, 1914
   Helping Himself
   The Good for Nothing
The Rounders, 1914
   The Love Thief

Two of a Kind
Oh, What a Night!
Tip, Tap, Toe
The New Janitor, 1914
  The New Porter
  The Blundering Boob
  The Porter
Those Love Pangs, 1914
  The Rival Mashers
  Busted Hearts
Dough and Dynamite, 1914
  The Cook
  The Doughnut Designer
  The New Cook
Gentlemen of Nerve, 1914
  Some Nerve
  Charlie at the Races
His Musical Career, 1914
  The Piano Movers
  Musical Tramps
His Trysting Place, 1914
  Family Home
  Family House
Tillie's Punctured Romance, 1914
  Tillie's Big Romance
  Tillie's Nightmare
  For the Love of Tillie
Getting Acquainted, 1914
  A Fair Exchange
  Exchange is no Robbery
His New Job, 1915
  Charlie's New Job
A Night Out, 1915
  Champagne Charlie

The Champion, 1915
  Battling Charlie
  Champion Charlie
In the Park, 1915
  Charlie in the Park
  Charlie in the Spree
The Jitney Elopement, 1915
  Charlie's Elopement
  Married in Haste
The Tramp, 1915
  Charlie the Hobo
By the Sea, 1915
  Charlie's Day Out
Work 1915
  Charlie at Work
  The Paperhanger
  The Plumber
  Only a Working Man
A Woman, 1915
  The Perfect Lady
The Bank, 1915
  Charlie Detective
  Charlie at the Bank
Shangaied, 1915
  Charlie the Sailor
A Night at the Show, 1915
  Charlie at the Show
Carmen, 1916
  Charlie Chaplin's Burlesque on Carmen
Police, 1916
  Housebreaker
  Charlie the Burglar
The Floorwalker, 1916
  The Store

Woody Allen

The films of Woody Allen:

What's New Pussycat?, 1965, UA
What's Up, Tiger Lily, 1966, AI
Casino Royale, 1967, Columbia
Take the Money and Run, 1969, Cinerama
Play It Again, Sam, 1972, Paramount
Everything You Always Wanted to Know About Sex
(But Were Afraid to Ask), 1972, UA
Sleeper, 1973, UA
Love and Death, 1975, UA
The Front, 1976, UA
Annie Hall, 1977, UA
Manhattan, 1979, UA
Stardust Memories, 1980, UA
A Midsummer Night's Sex Comedy, 1982, Orion Pictures
Zelig, 1983, Orion Pictures
Broadway Danny Rose, 1984, Orion Pictures
Hannah and Her Sisters, 1986, 20th Century-Fox

Bibliography

The Total Film-Maker
Jerry lewis
Warner Books, New York, 1973

King of Comedy
Mack Sennett and Cameron Shipp
Pinnacle Books, New York, 1975

The Crazy Mirror
Raymond Durgnat
Faber and Faber, London, 1969

Hooray! For Hollywood
Jim Heimann
Chronicle Books, San Francisco, 1983

The Explorer Magazine (Dutch Edition)
Pict Schreuders
Explorer Publishing, Amsterdam, 1986

Nieuw Weekblad voor de Cinematografie
Pier Westerbaan
The Hague, 1930-40/1945-50

Kinematograph Yearbook 1935-52
Odhams Press, London

International Motion Picture Almanac
Terry Ramsaye, Charles, S. Aaronson
Quigley Publishing, New York, 1945-55

Starmaker
Hal Wallis and Charles Higham
Macmillan Publishing, New York, 1980

Strangers in Paradise
John Russell Taylor
Faber and Faber, London, 1983

Charles Barr
Ealing Studios
Cameron & Tayleur, London, 1977

Forever Ealing
George Perry
Pavilion, London, 1981

RKO: The Biggest Little Major Of Them All
Betty Lasky
Prentice-Hall, Englewood Cliffs, 1984

The Armchair Odeon
Denis Gifford
Fountain Press, Hempstead, 1974

The MGM Stock Company
James Robert Parish and Ronald L. Bowers
Ian Allan, Shepperton, 1973

Some Time in the Sun
Tom Dardis
Charles Scribner's Sons, New York, 1976

The Hollywood Studios
Roy Pickard
Frederick Muller, London, 1978

The Parade's Gone By...
Kevin Brownlow
Bonanza Books, New York, 1969

The Long View
Basil Wright
Alfred A. Knopf, New York, 1974

Dream Palaces
Charles Lockwood
Viking Press, New York, 1981

Index